celtic meditations

Moments of

Thanksgiving,

Invitations to

Eucharist

by edward j. farrell

DIMENSION BOOKS

DENVILLE, NEW JERSEY

DEDICATION

To my Mother, Sarah Spellman Farrell,
in her seventy-fifth year, as a token of gratitude
for the faith, love and heritage she gives to me.

"Pray Always," "Traveling," "Sitting," "Sleeping" and
"Walking" are reprinted from *The Father Is Very Fond
of Me;* "Darkness," "Food," "Feet" and "Fire" from
Disciples and Other Strangers; "Object Meditation,"
"Hand Meditation," "Abandonment" and "Adoration"
from *Surprised by the Spirit.*

Published by

DIMENSION BOOKS
Denville, New Jersey

In general, the Scripture quotations are from
The Jerusalem Bible, published by Doubleday
and Company, and Darton Longman Todd to
whom grateful acknowledgement is hereby
made; but in certain instances for purposes of
clarification there is a slight divergence from
the text of the translations.

Table of Contents

INTRODUCTION

These meditations are called "Celtic" because they echo the ancient prayer of St. Patrick, "Christ with me, Christ before me, Christ behind me." They might also be called Meditations on the Sacramentals, a collection of blessings and prayers from the things of everyday.

> Through him all things came to be,
>   not one thing had its being but through him (Jn 1:2).
>
> It was you who created my inmost self,
>   and put me together in my mother's womb;
>   for all these mysteries I thank you:
>   for the wonder of myself, for the wonder of your
>   works (Ps 139:13).

Everything that is, has come from him, draws us back to him. Every being carries something of his imprint upon it. Everything holds within itself an intimation of him. Everything radiates something of his glory, his mystery, his love. Everything invites us to contemplate, to listen to its hidden prayer.

> I mean to sing to the Lord all my life. I mean to play for my God as long as I live. May these reflections of mine give him pleasure, as much as the Lord gives me (Ps 104:33).
>
> These he brought to man to see what he would call them; each one was to bear the name the man would give it (Gn 2:19).

To name is to contemplate, to experience the glory of God, to recognize God giving himself to man, the God whom no one can see, making himself visible, present to his people.

> God saw all that he had made and indeed it was very good (Gn 1:31).

Jesus, in offering himself, in offering bread and wine, is returning to the Father the whole of creation, transformed and made whole -holy.

Source of life and goodness, you have created all things to fill your creatures with every blessing and lead all men to the joyful vision of your light . . . and in the name of every creature under heaven we too praise your glory as we sing HOLY, HOLY, HOLY.

We shall sing your glory with every creature through Christ our Lord, through whom you give us everything that is good.   —IV Eucharistic Prayer.

The sacramentals are radiations of the one Sacrament, Jesus, the love of the Father for us, reflecting, inviting, calling us to worship, adoration, contemplation, prayer. The Eucharist, the light, the radiance of Jesus loving us unto death and resurrection, illuminates, transfigures all of creation. "He passed by and by his look alone clothed them with his glory" (John of the Cross).

These meditations are invitations, suggestions, possibilities, opportunities to listen, reflect, discover, create. Here is the Word of God focused on the things of everyday, so close to us, so much a part of our lives that we rarely advert to them. These are Scripture meditations, human words filled with the Divine Spirit.

The Word of God is something alive and active: it cuts like any double-edged sword, but more finely: it can slip through the place where the soul is divided from the spirit, or joints from the marrow; it can judge the secret emotions and thoughts (Heb 4:12).

Ever since you were a child, you have known the Holy Scriptures — from these you can learn wisdom that leads to salvation through faith in Christ Jesus. All scripture is inspired by God and can profitably be used for teaching, for refuting error, for guiding people's lives and teaching them to be holy. This is how the man who is dedicated to God becomes fully equipped and ready for any good work (2 Tim 3:15).

6

THE BREASTPLATE OF ST. PATRICK

I arise today through a mighty strength, the invocation of the Trinity, through a belief in the Threeness, through confession of the Oneness towards the Creator.

Christ to protect me today against poison, against burning, against drowning, against wounding, so that there may come abundance of reward.

Christ with me, Christ before me, Christ behind me,

Christ in me, Christ beneath me, Christ above me,

Christ on my right, Christ on my left,

Christ where I lie, Christ where I sit,

Christ where I arise,

Christ in the heart of every man who thinks of me,

Christ in the mouth of every man who speaks of me,

Christ in every eye that sees me,

Christ in every ear that hears me.

PSALM 104

The glories of creation

Bless Yahweh, my soul.
Yahweh my God, how great you are!
Clothed in majesty and glory,
wrapped in a robe of light!

You stretch the heavens out like a tent,
you build your palace on the waters above;
using the clouds as your chariot,
you advance on the wings of the wind;
you use the winds as messenger
and fiery flames as servants.

You fixed the earth on its foundations,
unshakeable for ever and ever;
you wrapped it with the deep as with a robe,
the waters overtopping the mountains.

At your reproof the waters took to flight,
they fled at the sound of your thunder,
cascading over the mountains, into the valleys,
down to the reservoir you made for them;
you imposed the limits they must never cross
    again,
or they would once more flood the land.

You set springs gushing in ravines,
running down between the mountains,
supplying water for wild animals,
attracting the thirsty wild donkeys;
near there the birds of the air make their nests
and sing among the branches.

From your palace you water the uplands
until the ground has had all that your heavens
    have to offer;
you make fresh grass grow for cattle

and those plants made use of by man,
for them to get food from the soil:
wine to make them cheerful,
oil to make them happy
and bread to make them strong.

The trees of Yahweh get rain enough,
those cedars of Lebanon he planted;
here the little birds build their nest
and, on the highest branches, the stork has its
    home.
For the wild goats there are the mountains,
in the crags rock-badgers hide.

You made the moon to tell the seasons,
the sun knows when to set:
you bring darkness on, night falls,
all the forest animals come out:
savage lions roaring for their prey,
claiming their food from God.

The sun rises, they retire,
going back to lie down in their lairs,
and man goes out to work,
and to labour until dusk.
Yahweh, what variety you have created,
arranging everything so wisely!

Earth is completely full of things you have made:
among them vast expanse of ocean,
teeming with countless creatures,
creatures large and small,
with the ships going to and fro
and Leviathan whom you made to amuse you.

All creatures depend on you
to feed them throughout the year;
you provide the food they eat,
with generous hand you satisfy their hunger.

You turn your face away, they suffer,
you stop their breath, they die
and revert to dust.
You give breath, fresh life begins,
you keep renewing the world.

Glory for ever to Yahweh!
May Yahweh find joy in what he creates,
at whose glance the earth trembles,
at whose touch the mountains smoke!   (1-32)

THE SUN

God said: Let there be light, and there was light (Gn 1:3).

God made the two great lights: the greater light to govern the day and the smaller light to govern the night (Gn 1:16).

High above, he pitches a tent for the sun, who comes out of his pavilion like a bridegroom exulting like a hero to run his race (Ps 19:5).

Pride of the heights, shining vault, so, in a glorious spectacle, the sky appears. The sun, as he emerges, proclaims at his rising, 'A thing of wonder is the work of the Most High!' At his zenith he parches the land, who can withstand his blaze? A man must blow a furnace to produce any heat, the sun burns the mountains three times as much; breathing out blasts of fire, flashing his rays he dazzles the eyes. Great is the Lord who made him, and whose word speeds him on his course. And then the moon, always punctual, to mark the months and make division of time: the moon it is that signals the feasts, a luminary that wanes after her full. The month derives its name from hers, she waxes wonderfully in her phases, banner of the hosts on high, shining in the vault of heaven. The glory of the stars makes the beauty of the sky, a brilliant decoration to the heights of the Lord. At the words of the Holy One they stand as he decrees, and never grow slack at their watch. See the rainbow and praise its maker, so superbly beautiful in its spendour. Across the sky it forms a glorious arc drawn by the hands of the Most High (Si 43:1-13).

Your Father in heaven, for he causes his sun to rise on bad men as well as good (Mt 5:45).

There in their presence he was transfigured: his face shone like the sun and his clothes became as white as the light (Mt 17:2).

Who from on high will bring the rising Sun to visit us, to give the light to those who live in darkness and the shadow of death (Lk 1:79).

The Word was the true light that enlightens all men (Jn 1:9).

That life was the light of men, a light that shines in the dark, a light that darkness could not overpower (Jn 1:5).

While you still have the light, believe in the light and you will become sons of light (Jn 12:36).

Never let the sun set on your anger (Ep 4:27).

And Christ will shine on you (Ep 5:14).

. . . God who called you out of the darkness into his wonderful light (1 P 2:9).

. . . Take it as a lamp for lighting a way through the dark until the dawn comes and the morning star rises in your minds (2 P 1:19).

But if we live our lives in the light, as he is in the light, we are in union with one another (1 Jn 1:7).

Because the night is over and the real light is already shining . . . anyone who loves his brother is living in the light (1 Jn 2:8).

And I will give him the Morning Star (Rv 2:28).

Now a great sign appeared in heaven: a woman, adorned with the sun, standing on the moon, and with twelve stars on her head for a crown (Rv 12:1).

And the city did not need the sun or the moon for light, since it was lit by the radiant glory of God and the Lamb was a lighted torch for it (Rv 21:23).

It will never be night again and they will not need lamplight or sunlight, because the Lord God will be shining on them (Rv 22:5).

"Who from on high will bring the rising sun to visit us, to give light to those who live in darkness and the shadow of death."

The gentleness of dawn! No one can hear the dawn, so deep its silence. As carefully as I may watch, I cannot catch the dawn. Darkness melts, steals away, light filters in everywhere all at once.

The sun plays games for little children, laughing its way through a window, reflecting, dancing its light off every mirror and reflector, creating rainbows on the ceilings, bouncing shadows off the wall.

The sun kisses every face (how I envy it), lifts up every heart, teases forth an irresistible smile, warms even the blind. How faithful the sun in winter. It is the special possession of the poor, sometimes their only friend, their only consolation, revealing rainbows in broken pieces of glass.

There is something of the primitive sunworshipper in every person, something of the Aztec, the Egyptian. The dawning sun has drawn the first deep sense of awe and wonder from countless hearts. And how many have been taken up into quieter, more intimate prayer, lost in the last lingering rays of the setting sun. It is a wonder that there are not more worshippers of the sun.

Artificial light, heat, energy make us forget how totally dependent we are on the sun. Suppose for one day that the sun failed to rise and the earth failed to turn into it. "All the darkness of the earth is created by its own shadow." It is the sun which holds the earth in its orbit, generating all the growth and energy which continues the earth's life. How long it takes to discover the gift and miracle of the sun. How long before it becomes prayer and sacrament!

How faithful the sun even in our ignorance and ununderstanding! How tired the sun must be — of our weary history of sin, war, inhumanity — from Adam and Eve until our own day, from Cain and Abel to you and me.

What joy when the same sun looked upon the Son of Man! And what joy when something of his image is reflected in us!

The sun has its unique splendor in each season, in winter snow and summer shimmers; in autumn leaves and spring flowers.

The sun companions us each day of our lives, in childhood and old age, in joy and in tragedy. How differently it touches us in every stage of life.

Each day the sun unites all nations under one light. Each day it touches the whole world, from mountain to mountain, ocean to ocean, from the Rockies to the Himalayas, to the Alps, to the Andes; from Pacific, to Indian, to Mediterranean,to Atlantic, to Arctic. Each day the same sun plays on every mountain, dances on every ocean.

Each day the sun gives its blessing to every city, to every home.

The sun is the original "mandala," the universal sphere and circle of completeness, totality, perfection. The sun is the most universal symbol, conscious and unconscious, the most attractive and pleasing of aesthetic forms and figures: moon, earth, tear and dewdrop, mouth and eye, the spheres and curves of the human body, the circle of human embrace. Sun, earth, Eucharistic host intermingle their universal orbits.

Jesus fulfills the richest symbolism of the sun in Resurrection. It is what the sun had been waiting for since the dawn of creation. Matthew, "And toward dawn." Mark, "And very early in the morning." Luke, "At the first sign of dawn." "Jesus rose from the dead," a "light that shines in the dark, a light that darkness could not overpower" (Jn 1:5). The sun is the daily promise that he has overcome the world of darkness, sin and death, and that "he is coming soon" (Rv 22:20), that already "I am standing at the door, knocking" (Rv 3:20). The sun heralds the daily Eucharist. "From the rising of the sun to its setting my name is honored among the nations and everywhere a sacrifice of incense is offered to my name." The sun is the first candle on every altar, the sanctuary lamp of the sky. Every dawn is exposition, every setting is reposition, the eternal fire and light inviting us "Come, let us adore him."

BREATH, AIR, WIND, SPIRIT

And God's spirit hovered over the water (Gn 1:2).

Yahweh God fashioned man of dust from the soil. Then he breathed into his nostrils a breath of life, and thus man became a living being (Gn 2:7).

Put into me a new and constant spirit . . . do not deprive me of your holy spirit . . . keep my spirit ready and willing . . . my sacrifice is this broken spirit (Ps 51). Remembering they were creatures of flesh, a breath that passes and does not return (Ps 78:39).

You stop their breath, they die and revert to dust. You give breath, fresh life begins, you keep renewing the world (Ps 104:29).

Where could I go to escape your Spirit, where could I flee from your presence? (Ps 139:7).

And then you endowed me with life, watched each breath of mine with tender care (Jb 10:12).

15

Were he to recall his breath to draw his breathing back into himself, things of flesh would disappear all together and man would return to dust (Jb 34:14).

The spirit of the Lord indeed fills the whole world (Ws 1:7).

Who could have learned it had you not granted Wisdom and sent your holy spirit from above (Ws 9:17).

The dust returns to the earth as it once came from it and the breath of God who gave it (Qo 12:7).

I will put a new spirit in them; I will remove the heart of stone from their bodies and give them a heart of flesh instead (Ezk 12:19).

And brings the wind out of his storehouse (Ps 135:7).

He sends his word to bring the thaw and warm wind to melt the snow (Ps 147:18).

You carry me up to ride the wind, tossing me about in a tempest (Jb 30:22).

There came a mighty wind, so strong it tore the mountains and shattered the rocks before Yahweh. But Yahweh was not in the wind. After the wind came an earthquake, but Yahweh was not in the earthquake. After the earthquake came a fire. But Yahweh was not in the fire. And after the fire there came the sound of a gentle breeze (1 K 19:11).

And he awoke and rebuked the wind . . . and the wind stopped and all was calm again . . . Even the wind and sea obey him (Mk 5:39).

Then he got into the boat with them and the wind stopped (Mk 7:51).

The wind blows wherever it pleases; you hear its sound, but you cannot tell where it comes from or where it is going. That is how it is with all who are born of the Spirit (Jn 3:8).

After saying this he breathed on them and said, "Receive the Holy Spirit" (Jn 20:22).

When suddenly they heard what sounded like a powerful wind from heaven, the noise of which filled the entire house in which they were sitting (Ac 2:2).

The finest poem in the English language on "air" is Gerard Manley Hopkins' unparalleled masterpiece, "The Blessed Virgin Compared to the Air we Breathe."

Wild air, world-mothering air,
Nestling me everywhere,
That each eyelash or hair
Girdles; goes home betwixt
The fleecrest, frailest-flixed
Snowflake; that's fairly mixed
With, riddles, and is rife
In every least thing's life;
This needful, never spent,
And nursing element;
My more than meat and drink,
My meal at every wink;
This air, which, by life's law,
By being must draw and draw
Now but to breathe its praise.

* * *

Above me, round me lie
Fronting my froward eye
With sweet and scarless sky;
Stir in my ears, speak there
Of God's love, O live air,
Of patience, penance, prayer
World-mothering air, air wild
Wound with thee, in thee is led
Fold home, fast fold thy child.

The Hebrews had no concept for our word "soul." For them, the principle of life was the "ruah," the breath of God. God fashioned man of dust from the soil. Then he breathed into his nostrils a breath of life and thus man became a living being. The "ruah" always remained God's. When man died, his body returned to the earth, but his "ruah" returned to God. What deep intuition! I live because he breathes in me. He is the breath of my breath, the Spirit of my spirit. This is the key to "the mystery that has now been revealed through the Spirit to his holy apostles and prophets and unknown to any men in past generations . . . the infinite treasure of Christ . . . through all the ages, this has been kept hidden in God, the creator of everything" (Ep 3:5-9).

Breathing is the most basic sign of life outside the womb. However, the most essential activities are usually those least recognized and reflected upon. As children, we discovered our breath in the first cold days of winter when we could breathe a frosty breath. In learning to swim, mastery began when we could hold our breath underwater. Running and playing strenuously "shortened" our breath or we simply "ran" out of breath. In preparing to fall asleep at night we listened and learned the rhythm of our own breathing, the quietest, the most gentle of all of life's rhythms.

How quickly we became aware of city air in contrast to country air; the "light" air of the mountains, the "heavy" air of the ocean; the tired air of night, the fresh air of morning; the dancing air of May, the sharp, chill, piercing air of December. "The wind blows wherever it pleases. You hear its sound but you cannot tell where it comes from or where it is going. That is how it is with all who are born of the Spirit" (Jn 3:8). The winter and spring winds are the child's first experience of mystery, transcendence beyond his vocabulary and beyond the vocabulary of his parents.

Who can name the wind? Wind overpowers the voices of men and commands their silence. The wind is the breath of God's power and compels man's reverence. What is more powerful than a hurricane or tornado sweeping up everything in its path? What is more gentle than the caress of a Spring breeze? Such is our God!

The air is catholic and common; we share it with all of life, people, animals, trees, vegeta-

tion, mountains, the earth itself. Into this common air Jesus came. He breathed our breath. And now we breathe his breath, not merely the breath of the lungs, but the breath of the Spirit. In giving us his Spirit, he has breathed into us an eternal breath. The "breath" he gives is his risen life. As the "last Adam," Jesus in his resurrection becomes the "life-giving Spirit" (1 Co 15:46). "And we, with our unveiled faces reflecting like mirrors the brightness of the Lord, all grow brighter and brighter as we are turned into the image that we reflect; this is the work of the Lord who is Spirit" (2 Co 3:18). And thus "all life, all holiness comes from you through your Son, Jesus Christ our Lord, by the working of the Holy Breath" (III Eucharistic Prayer).

EARTH

God saw all that he had made and indeed it was very good (Gn 1:31).

Yahweh God fashioned man of dust from the soil. Then he breathed into his nostrils a breath of life, and thus man became a living being (Gn 2:7).

Yahweh God took the man and settled him in the garden of Eden to cultivate it and take care of it (Gn 2:16).

Accursed be the soil because of you. With suffering shall you get your food from it every day of your life (Gn 3:17).

For dust you are and to dust you shall return (Gn 3:19).

The Lord said to him, "Take off your shoes; the place where you are standing is holy ground" (Ex 3:5; Ac 7:33).

To Yahweh belong earth and all it holds, the world and all who live in it (Ps 24:1).

The earth is full of the goodness of God (Ps 33:5).

You visit the earth and water it, you load it with riches (Ps 65:9).

Acclaim God, all the earth, play music to the glory of

his name . . . *all the earth bows down to you (Ps 66:1).*

May the whole earth be filled with his glory (Ps 72:19).

Let earth rejoice . . . let the fields exult and all that is in them, let all the woodland trees cry out for joy (Ps 96:11).

All the ends of the earth have seen the saving power of our God. Acclaim Yahweh, all the earth, burst into shouts of joy (Ps 98:4).

God, what variety you have created, arranging everything so wisely! Earth is completely full of things you have made (Ps 104:24).

You give breath, fresh life begins, you keep renewing the world (Ps 104:30).

Then he instructed the crowd to sit down on the ground (Mt 15:36).

He spit on the ground, made clay with the spittle, put this over the eyes of the blind man, and said to him, "Go and wash" (Jn 9:6).

But Jesus bent down and started writing on the ground with his finger . . . Then he bent down and wrote on the ground again (Jn 8:6).

And the one who receives the seed in rich soil is the man who hears the word and understands it; he is the one who yields a harvest and produces now a hundredfold, now sixty, now thirty (Mt 13:23).

As for the part in the good earth, this is people with a noble and generous heart who have heard the word and take it to themselves and yield a harvest through their perseverance (Lk 8:15).

I tell you, most solemnly, unless a wheat grain falls into the earth and dies, it remains only a single grain, but if it dies, it yields a rich harvest (Jn 12:24).

And going on a little further he threw himself on the ground and prayed . . . (Mk 14:35).

In his anguish he prayed even more earnestly, and his sweat fell to the ground like great drops of blood (Lk 22:24).

The earth quaked; the rocks were split (Mt 27:52).

Took Jesus down from the cross, wrapped him in the shroud and laid him in a tomb which had been hewn out of the rock (Mk 15:46).

He fell to the ground and then he heard a voice saying, "Saul, Saul, why are you persecuting me?" (Ac 9:4).

I watched it intently and saw all sorts of animals and

wild beasts—everything possible that could walk, crawl or fly. Then I heard a voice that said to me, "Now Peter, kill and eat . . . What God has made clean, you have no right to call profane" (Ac 10:12).

Ever since God created the world his everlasting power and deity — however invisible — have been there for the mind to see in the things he has made (Rm 1:20). The whole creation is on tiptoe to see the wonderful sight of the sons of God coming into their own. It was not for any fault on the part of creation that it was made unable to attain its purpose . . . but creation still retains the hope of being freed, like us, from the tyranny of change and decay, to enjoy that magnificent freedom which can only belong to the children of God. From the beginning till now the entire creation, as we know, has been groaning in one great act of giving birth." (Rm 8:19-22).

What we are waiting for is what he promised: the new heavens and the new earth (2 P 3:13).

Then I saw a new heaven and a new earth (Rv 21:1).

Earth . . . the good earth . . . "mother" earth. What instinctive reverence we have for the earth. The echo of the words spoken to Moses never entirely fade away, "Take off your shoes: the place where you are standing is holy ground." The Hindus have a saying, "Take off your shoes and the ground becomes holy." How differently we see and use the earth, the farmer and the road builder; the poet, the grave-digger; the gardener, the child!

How close the child to earth! What delight, joy,we take in the creativity of our clay and sand. How affectionate the earth to little children, clinging, penetrating, embedding itself so totally that mothers wonder with exasperation where earth ends and child begins. How lovingly the earth "mothers," delights, fondles little children. It embraces the child as does the Wisdom of Proverbs, "I was by his side . . . delighting him day by day, ever at play in his presence, at play everywhere in his world, delighting to be with the sons of men" (Pr 8:30). How we loved as children to roll in the grass or to roll down a slope. The joy of digging into the earth in endless exploration, burying one's face and arms in the earth to hug it!

The earth is alive and living. It breathes as you and I breathe. It breathes from ocean floor to mountain top whether covered with glacier or paved with asphalt. The earth continues to grow, lifting up mountains, deepening, renewing itself; valleys growing old yet giving new birth, older than old but as new as today.

"God, what variety you have created, arranging everything so wisely. Earth is completely full of the things you have made."

"You give breath, fresh life begins, You keep renewing the earth." Untiringly the earth continues to nourish us; richly, profusely, she feeds us. How hungrily we devour her each day of our life as she nourishes us faithfully with her very own life.

The same earth gives birth to great variety from the blade of grass to the thousand-year-old redwood. The immensity of life she supports, ever giving, ever receiving back.

The earth has its own laws and rhythms. We must learn them and respect them. We do not discipline the earth; earth disciplines us. We do not recycle the earth; the earth recycles us. Ash Wednesday is truly *Earth* Wednesday.

The earth teaches us to breathe, enables us to breathe. Wherever we go into space, we must take the earth with us for we cannot survive without it. We are as rooted in the earth as a giant redwood; as immersed in its atmosphere as a whale in the ocean.

The movement of the earth, rotating her face before the sun a thousand miles an hour, orbiting the sun each year in its 186-million-mile radius!

How patiently the earth carries our footprints, handprints all the days of our life. How tenderly she waits for us to come to rest, to sleep within her forever, returning to her the earth we have received from her.

How holy the earth has become because it has been inspirited by our consciousness. How good it is to know that Jesus has experienced each of our earth experiences, continuing to do so each day as we offer him the bread, "fruit of the earth and work of human hands," and the "wine, fruit of the vine and work of human hands."

WATER

There was darkness over the deep, and God's spirit hovered over the water (Gn 1:2).

A river flowed from Eden to water the garden, and from there it divided to make four streams (Gn 2:10).

I mean to make it rain on the earth for forty days and nights, and I will rid the earth of every living thing that I made . . . and his heart grieved (Gn 7:4).

Yahweh drove back the sea with a strong easterly wind all night and he made dry land of the sea. The waters parted and the sons of Israel went on dry land right into the sea, walls of water to right and to left of them (Ex 14:21).

You must strike the rock, and water will flow from it for the people to drink (Ex 17:6).

To the water of repose he leads me, there he revives my soul (Ps 23:2).

24

As a doe longs for running streams . . . my soul thirsts for God, the God of my life (Ps 42:2).

My soul is thirsting for you . . . as a land parched, weary and waterless (Ps 63:2).

Like thirsty ground, I long for you (Ps 143:6).

Drink the water from your own cistern, fresh water from your own well (Pr 5:15).

I will make rivers well up on barren heights and fountains in the midst of valleys, turn the wilderness into a lake and dry ground into watersprings (Is 41:18).

For I pour out water on the thirsty soil, streams on dry ground. I will pour my spirit on your descendants, my blessings on your children. They shall grow like grass where there is plenty of water, like poplars by running streams (Is 44:3).

Oh, come to the water all you who are thirsty (Is 55:1).

They have abandoned me, the fountain of living water, only to dig cisterns for themselves, leaky cisterns that hold no water (Jr 2:13).

Those who turn from you will be uprooted from the land, since they have abandoned the fountain of living water (Jr 17:13).

As soon as Jesus was baptized he came up from the water (Mt 3:16).

If anyone gives so much as a cup of cold water to one of these little ones because he is a disciple, then I tell you solemnly, he will most certainly not lose his reward (Mt 10:42).

And when the disciples saw him walking on the lake they were terrified . . . if it is you, tell me to come across the water. "Come," said Jesus (Mt 14:6).

Simon . . . you poured no water over my feet (Lk 7:44).

Then he woke up and rebuked the wind and the rough water (Lk 8:24).

Fill the jars with water . . . the steward tasted the water and it had turned into wine (Jn 2:7).

Unless a man is born through water and the Spirit he cannot enter the kingdom of God (Jn 3:5).

Anyone who drinks the water that I shall give will never be thirsty again: the water I shall give will turn into a spring inside him, welling up to eternal life (Jn 4:14).

If any man is thirsty, let him come to me. Let the man come and drink who believes in me. As Scripture says: From his breast shall flow fountains of living water (Jn 7:37).

And he poured water into a basin and began to wash his disciples' feet (Jn 13:5). . . . .

One of the soldiers pierced his side with a lance, and immediately there came out blood and water (Jn 19:34).

He made her clean by washing her in water with a form of words (Ep 5:26).

Jesus Christ who came by water and blood, not with water only, but with water and blood (1 Jn 5:6).

The Lamb . . . will be their shepherd and will lead them to springs of living water (Rv 7:17).

I will give water from the well of life free to anyone who is thirsty (Rv 21:6).

The river of life, rising from the throne of God and of the Lamb and flowing crystal clear down the middle of the city (Rv 22:1).

Water is the universal source and medium of life, so universal that we take it for granted. Each of us began our existence in the ocean of embryonic waters within our mother's womb, and it is out of these waters that we are born. Soon after our natural birth we are born again in the womb of the Christian community through the power of God's spirit hovering over the waters of baptism. We are plunged, "baptized," immersed in the Father, Son and Holy Spirit. "And the water I will give will turn into a living spring inside of him, welling up to eternal life."

It is no wonder that we are fascinated by water! We experience a gravitational attraction to water, which is both physical and psychological, conscious and unconscious. The major component of our human body is water (90%). Most of our food follows the same pattern with a high percentage of solids being water. Water covers three-fourths of our globe. And from the moon, the earth appears as a blue diamond because of its water.

Without water there would be no life. And

much of our life is related to water! Water is the most human, the most universal thirst quencher; all other liquids are but modified or "treated" water; their basic content and *value* is water: beer, soft, hard drinks, etc.

The joy and refreshment of water: washing, bathing, cleaning, showering, swimming.

All the beauty that water reveals to us in ocean, river, lake, waterfall. All the different forms that water can assume: ice, frost, hail, snow; dew, moisture, mist, fog; steam, humidity, dampness. Think of all of the different kinds of rain, and with rain, the rainbow. Think of clouds and cloud formations. All of our weather is basically the presence or absence of water. Without water, weather would not exist; we would simply have sun and wind and absence of life as on the moon and other planets.

Water is man's most intimate friend. At the same time, too much or too little water can have devastating effects. The floods and deserts continue to take their toll. Gales, tornadoes, hurricanes, typhoons illustrate graphically the destructive force of water.

Water is the most perfect mirror of God's creation and grace. He calls us to meditate with himself the depth, the height, the secret, sacrament, mystery of water. His tears of joy, his tears of sorrow; the sweat of blood, the heart pierced from which flowed "blood and water." Our own tears of joy, our tears of sorrow. The sweat of fear and anxiety; the sweat of hard work, holy sweat, holy water drawn from our bodies in loving service for others.

CANTICLE OF THE
THREE YOUNG MEN

'All things the Lord has made, bless the Lord:
give glory and eternal praise to him.
Angels of the Lord! all bless the Lord:
give glory and eternal praise to him.
Heavens! bless the Lord:
give glory and eternal praise to him.
Waters above the heavens! bless the Lord:
give glory and eternal praise to him.
Powers of the Lord! all bless the Lord:
give glory and eternal praise to him.
Sun and moon! bless the Lord:
give glory and eternal praise to him.
Stars of heaven! bless the Lord:
give glory and eternal praise to him.
Showers and dews! all bless the Lord:
give glory and eternal praise to him.
Winds! all bless the Lord:
give glory and eternal praise to him.
Fire and heat! bless the Lord:
give glory and eternal praise to him.
Cold and heat! bless the Lord:
give glory and eternal praise to him.
Dews and sleets! bless the Lord:
give glory and eternal praise to him.
Frost and cold! bless the Lord:
give glory and eternal praise to him.
Ice and snow! bless the Lord:
give glory and eternal praise to him.

Nights and days! bless the Lord:
give glory and eternal praise to him.
Light and darkness! bless the Lord:
give glory and eternal praise to him.
Lightning and clouds! bless the Lord:
give glory and eternal praise to him.
Let the earth bless the Lord,
give glory and eternal praise to him.
Mountains and hills! bless the Lord:
give glory and eternal praise to him.
Every thing that grows on the earth! bless the
    Lord:
give glory and eternal praise to him.
Springs of water! bless the Lord:
give glory and eternal praise to him.
Seas and rivers! bless the Lord:
give glory and eternal praise to him.
Sea beasts and everything that lives in water!
    bless the Lord:
give glory and eternal praise to him.
Birds of heaven! all bless the Lord:
give glory and eternal praise to him.
Animals wild and tame! all bless the Lord:
give glory and eternal praise to him.
Sons of men! bless the Lord:
give glory and eternal praise to him.
Israel! bless the Lord:
give glory and eternal praise to him.
Priests! bless the Lord:
give glory and eternal praise to him.
Servants of the Lord! bless the Lord:

give glory and eternal praise to him.
Spirits and souls of the virtuous! bless the Lord:
give glory and eternal praise to him.
Devout and humble-hearted men! bless the
  Lord:
give glory and eternal praise to him.
Ananiah, Azariah, Mishael! bless the Lord:
give glory and eternal praise to him.
For he has snatched us from the underworld,
saved us from the hand of death,
saved us from the burning fiery furnace,
rescued us from the heart of the flame.
Give thanks to the Lord, for he is good,
for his love is everlasting.
All you who worship him, bless the God of gods,
praise him and give him thanks,
for his love is everlasting.'   (Dn 3:57-90)

LEARNING AND STUDY
KNOWLEDGE AND WISDOM
TRUTH AND HOLINESS-WHOLENESS

Man does not live by bread alone but on every word that comes from the mouth of God (Dt 8:3).

The mind of the just studieth obedience (Pr 15:28).

One last thing, my son, be warned that writing books involves endless hard work, and that much study wearies the body (Qo 12:12).

And so I prayed and understanding was given me; I entreated, and the spirit of Wisdom came to me (Ws 7:7).

On him the Spirit of Yahweh rests,
*   a spirit of wisdom and insight,*
*   a spirit of counsel and power*
*   a spirit of knowledge and the fear of Yahweh (Is 11:2).*

Do you know why I have come to you? It is to tell you what is written in the Book of Truth . . . And now I will tell you the truth about these things (Dn 10:20-11:2).

Go and learn the meaning of the words (Mt 9:13).

Shoulder my yoke and learn from me, for I am gentle and humble of heart, and you will find rest for your souls (Mt 11:29).

With the coming of the Sabbath he began teaching in the synagogue and most of them were astonished when they heard him. They said: "Where did the man get all this? What is this wisdom that has been granted him?" (Mk 6:2).

His Mother stored up all these things in her heart (Lk 2:52).

I myself shall give you an eloquence and a wisdom that none of your opponents will be able to resist or contradict (Lk 21:15).

In the beginning was the Word and the Word was with God (Jn 1:1).

Indeed, from his fulness we have, all of us, received . . . grace and truth have come through Jesus Christ (Jn 1:16).

To the Jews who believed in him Jesus said: "If you make my word your home you will indeed be my disciples, you will learn the truth and the truth will make you free" (Jn 8:31-32).

I am the Way, the Truth and the Life. No one can come

to the Father except through me. If you know me, you know my Father too (Jn 14:6-7).

But when the Spirit of truth comes he will lead you to the complete truth . . . (Jn 16:13).

. . . I was born for this, I came into the world for this: To bear witness to the truth; and all who are on the side of truth listen to my voice (Jn 18:37).

They found they could not get the better of him because of his wisdom, and because it was the Spirit that prompted what he said (Ac 6:10).

How rich are the depths of God — how deep his wisdom and knowledge and how impossible to penetrate his motives or understand his methods! (Rm 11:33).

If we live by the truth and in love, we shall grow in all ways into Christ . . . (Ep 4:15).

You were taught what the truth is in Jesus . . . Your mind must be renewed by a spiritual revolution so that you can put on the new self that has been created in God's way, in the goodness and holiness of the truth (Ep 4:23-24).

Let the message of Christ, in all its richness find a home with you. Teach each other, and advise each other, in all wisdom (Col 3: 16). .. ..

However, we do urge you, brothers, to go on making even greater progress (1 Th 4:11).

To do this is right, and will please God our Saviour; he wants everyone to be saved and reach full knowledge of the truth (1 Tm 2:4).

Think over what I have said, and the Lord will show you how to understand it all (2 Tm 2:7).

Do all you can to present yourself in front of God as a man who has come through his trials, and a man who has no cause to be ashamed of his life's work and has kept a straight course with the message of truth (2 Tm 2:15).

You must keep to what you have been taught and know to be true; remember who your teachers were, and how, ever since you were a child, you have known the holy scriptures — from these you can learn the wisdom that leads to salvation through faith in Christ Jesus. All scripture is inspired by God and can profitably be used for teaching, for refuting error, for guiding people's lives and teaching them to be holy. This is how the man who is dedicated to God becomes fully equipped and ready for any good work (2 Tm 3:14).

If there is any one of you who needs wisdom, he must ask God, who gives to all freely and ungrudgingly; it will be given to him (Jm 1:5).

If there are any wise or learned men among you, let them show it by their good lives, with humility and wisdom in their actions (Jm 3:15).

There are many deceivers in the world, refusing to admit that Jesus Christ has come in the flesh. They are the Deceiver; they are the antichrist. Watch yourselves, or all your work will be lost and not get the reward it deserves. If anybody does not keep within the teaching of Christ but goes beyond it, he cannot have God with him (2 Jn 7-9).

I had a thought! . . . imagine one single thought . . . a greater phenomenon than a sunrise or sunset, more marvelous than a snow-capped mountain, an endless ocean beach, a higher, deeper expression of life than all of creation! I had a thought. I understand. I saw the connection. I see!

Every moment of my life is a learning experience. Every person opens a new door, vista. Everything is a "come and see," come and eat, come and rest.

Who can begin to tell the adventures of one human mind. Who can begin to comprehend one's own stream of consciousness. It would be as difficult as trying to know the drops of water in an ocean. What an immense journey the exploration into the inner self, "where no thief can steal nor moth or rust corrupt." The never-to-be-completed task of the growth and development of our mind and heart, the length, breadth, height, depth of the continents, the oceans within. Eye has not seen nor ear heard what God is preparing for those who seek him.

When we were too young to work, i.e. to make money, perhaps we did the most important work of our lives, the growth and development of our learning, loving capacity. I remember a young student telling me that he had decided to study philosophy because he believed that he would use his mind for all eternity and he wanted to get a good head start.

How valuable our early years in school when we were invited into the mysteries of reading, writing, the travels of the mind, so much richer than any traveling of the feet. Teachers, each with their own gift, introducing us to the great books, the great ideas. Spiritual teachers, encouraging us to write, to explore our own mind and heart.

I think; therefore I am. My own mind and intelligence. How mysterious I am. I am a learning being with an infinite capacity. There is no end to learning, knowledge, to study, work, an endless winter, spring, summer, fall. "I seek to comprehend all knowledge. I ever struggle to hold within my grasp the mystery of being. I want the power of knowing all, of seeking all, of having all . . . but I cannot even possess myself."

> Now we are seeing in a mirror, but then we shall be seeing face to face. The knowledge that I have now is imperfect; but then I shall know as fully as I am known (1 Co 13:12).
> I have been holding forth on matters which I cannot understand, on marvels beyond me and my knowledge . . . I knew you then only by hearsay; but now, having seen you with my own eyes, I retract all I have said and in dust and ashes I repent (Jb 42:3).

My mind draws me into myself and out into the universe. The wonders of human inspiration, remembrance; of dream, fantasy. Pilgrim of the absolute, a mind in tune with Divinity. Mind over matter, over space and time. Ever learning, assimilating, recreating. Study. Research. Mind mastering mind. My mind and intelligence in dialogue with the great thinkers of all time.

All human knowledge whetting the mind. The mind is potentially the whole universe, ultimately God. Knowledge of the senses. Experience direct and immediate. Understanding. Knowing causes and destinies. Knowing history. Knowing people, relationships. The infinite expandability of the human mind.

Truth is a hunger. Truth is holy. Truth is wholeness. "I am . . . the truth." "If you make my word your home you will indeed be my disciples, you will learn the truth and the truth will make you free."

Study is the path to truth; truth makes the heart of man free, whole. The vocation to truth is a sacred call to study, to silence, to prayer. There is the prayer of the learner; there is the prayer of the teacher. Becoming a learner is a long journey of discipleship. "The learner is not self-begotten; he is begotten of the truth, of the creative Word" (Sertillanges).

The lover of wisdom, the seeker of truth, the pilgrim of the absolute is always overshadowed with the final prayer of Jesus: "Consecrate them in truth; your word is truth . . . and for their sake I consecrate myself so that they too may be consecrated in truth" (Jn 17:17).

DESERT, SILENCE, SOLITUDE

My Lord, Yahweh, Abraham replied, what do you in-tend to give me? (Gn 15:1).

The Lord led his people through the desert to bring them to a homeland. Desert was the way to the land flowing with milk and honey (Dt 1:9).

You will seek Yahweh your God from there, and if you seek him with all your heart and with all your soul, you shall find him (Dt 4:29).

You must not put the Lord your God to the test (Dt 6:16).

You must worship the Lord your God and serve him alone (Dt 6:16).

Man does not live on bread alone, but on every word that comes from the mouth of God (Dt 8:3).

God brought you out of Egypt, the place of slavery. He guided you through the vast and terrible desert with its serpents and scorpions; its parched and waterless ground. He brought forth water for you from the flinty rock and fed you in the desert with manna. He afflicted you and tested you but made you prosperous in the end (Dt 8:14-16).

A voice cries: prepare in the wilderness a way for Yahweh. Make a straight highway for our God across the desert (Is 40:3).

I remember the affection of your youth, the love of your bridal days. You followed me through the wilder-ness, through a land unsown (Jr 2:2).

Yahweh led his people through the desert, the land of water and gullies; land of drought and darkness, where no man dwelled — and brought him into garden land (Jr 2:6-7).

I looked, and behold . . . the garden land was a desert and all its cities destroyed (Jr 4:26).

When you seek me you shall find me, when you seek me with all your heart (Jr 29:13).

They have found pardon in the wilderness (Jr 31:2).

That is why I am going to lure her. I will allure her. I will lead her into the desert and speak to her heart . . . I will make a covenant. I will espouse you to me forever. I will espouse you in love and mercy. I will espouse you in fidelity and you shall know the Lord (Ho 2:16).

When Israel was a child I loved him and I called my son out of Egypt (Ho 11:1).

Immediately afterwards his spirit drove him out into the wilderness and he remained there for forty days and was tempted by Satan. He was with the wild beasts, and the angels looked after him (Mk 1:12).

He led the people out of Egypt, performing miracles and wonders in Egypt (Ac 7:36).

When they held the assembly in the wilderness . . . (Ac 7:38).

God brought them out of Egypt by his great power (Ac 13:17).

Their bodies were scattered over the desert (1 Co 10:5).

But I went off to Arabia at once (Ga 1:17).

In the desert the people rebelled against God, tempted him and put him to the test (Heb 3:8).

Because you have kept my plea to stand fast I will keep you safe in the time of trial (Rv 3:10).

And the child was taken straight away up to God and to his throne while the woman escaped into the desert where God had made a place of safety ready for her to be looked after in the twelve hundred and sixty days (Rv 12:6).

They follow the lamb wherever he goes (Rv 14:4).

To go to the desert is to return to beginnings. There is always a need for a new exodus, purification, conversion. The desert is essentially a test, a challenge to faith and providence, a self-confrontation with haunting words, "Can you drink the cup I have drunk?" — to be poor, to live on subsistence, to walk the edge of survival. In Genesis 2:8, Paradise is pictured as an oasis in the eastern desert. Amos, Hosea, Jeremiah regard the period in the desert as a time of perfect union between Yahweh and his people. The desert was a refuge. Hosea, like Amos before him, thought of Israel's journey through the desert as a time of spiritual idyll. Israel was then a child, knowing nothing of pagan gods, loyal to Yahweh whose presence was manifest in the cloud.

The desert is a place of paradox, a place of great confinement, sandy and sometimes grassy, bleak with great color, flat, still, and like a mighty, rising sea. The desert is parched and without water but there is always an oasis. It is the place of battle-danger, hardship, death; a place of refuge, solitude for the holy man and for the bandit. To lose one's way in the desert is almost certain death. A caravan that turns aside from the route in the desert will surely perish (Jb 6:18). The desert is the haunt of demons and wild animals. The desert is a place of passage, never a final place in itself. Desert was the way chosen by God to bring his people home. The desert is a place of adoration, worship, prayer, receiving law and covenant, a place of infidelity where people murmured, were without security, meat, water. Desert was also the place of mercy. The Lord gave water, food. Desert is a place of great safety, protection, refuge, the place where Israel found favor with God. The desert is the place of Jesus. He began his ministry in the desert. He was driven by the Spirit into the desert. In the desert, he overcame; he became the faithful one. The desert, the lonely place, is the special place of miracles. The desert is a provocative place; it evokes our latent taste for adventure, exploration, solitude.

What can you expect from the desert? What can you ask of the desert? What do you go out to the desert to see? Expect, hope. The promise of the desert is: an encounter with your devil, an encounter with the spring of living water. Strike a rock in your desert! Manna. Above all, expect manna in the desert. There is always manna. Expect a new name (Rv 2:17), a morning star (Rv 2:28), an open door (Rv 3:8). Yahweh, my God, is a desert God. He brings me to the desert within. In the deepest center of every person, there is a desert. You will not survive in the desert unless you affirm wholeheartedly its reality and come to terms with its severity. Man needs to stand in the scorched desert under the noonday sun and see things as they really are. Yahweh did not call his people into the desert for nothing, but for ALL, for the promised land. Jesus is the desert man, silent, solitary, going to the lonely place, the desert, the sea, the mountain, the city. The Father's absorbing, compelling presence empowered him. Far from some isolated episode, the desert was integrated into the whole of his mission. He was transfigured in the wilderness; the culmination of his desert took place at Calvary.

The physical desert is often inaccessible, but the desert experience is essential: Lent, retreat, holy hour, fasting, silence, thirst. Especially is Eucharist a desert. Each time and for each person the desert is new, unique. Deep in the desert of each person's spirit there is a secret. "If you wait long enough the desert will bloom, even in the night."

The desert is both geographical, a place, a land which God has not blessed, and privileged time, a place of passage. Christ is our desert. In him we have overcome the trial. In him we have perfect faithfulness, transformation, solitude, communion with God. Within each of us is that mysterious call to a life of direct communion with God, of dependence upon him, a call to be guided, formed, purified by him in silence, prayer, solitude, freedom.

41

Silence is sound from the future, an intimation of eternity. Eternity has begun for me. I carry eternity within me; it is slowly, silently growing out of me. More is becoming eternalized, forevered. "Whoever really possesses the Word of Jesus can sense also his silence" (Ignatius of Antioch). Silence is our way of going into the desert, into eternity.

> A breath slid over my face, the hairs of my body bristled. Someone stood there — I could not see his face, but the form remained before me. Silence — and then I heard a voice (Jb 4:16).

> My words have been frivolous: what can I reply? I had better lay my finger on my lips. I have spoken once . . . I will not speak again; more than once . . . I will add nothing (Jb 40:4).

> No utterance at all, no speech, no sound that anyone can hear; yet their voice goes out through all the earth and their message to the ends of the world (Ps 19:3).

> A time for keeping silent . . . (Qo 3:7).

> It is good to wait in silence for Yahweh to save, to sit in solitude and silence when the Lord fastens it on him (Lm 3:26).

> But Yahweh is in his holy temple. Let the whole earth be silent before him (Hab 2:20).

> Let all mankind be silent before Yahweh! For he is awakening and is coming from his holy dwelling (Zc 2:13).

> But when he was accused by the chief priests and the elders he refused to answer at all . . . But to the governor's complete amazement, he offered no reply to any of the charges (Mt 27:12).

> But he was silent and made no answer at all (Mk 14:61).

> The lamb then broke the seventh seal and there was silence in heaven for about half an hour (Rv 8:1).

We each carry our own depth of silence, the human kind of silence not found anywhere else. Another can enable us to discover the hidden silence within ourselves. It is a special gift to receive the depth silence of another. Silence is a presence, a receptivity, a readiness, a waiting, a listening. There are different kinds of silence, expressing contentment, fullness, or emptiness. Silence has many different faces, meanings. There is the silence of wisdom and the silence of ignorance, the silence of humility and the silence of poverty, the silence of anger and the silence of love. There is the silence of Jesus among men for thirty years, the silence of Nazareth, of Bethlehem, of the desert, of the nights on the mountain. There is the silence of nature, the turning of the earth, its movement around the sun, the silence of the sun, the moon, the stars, the ground. Noise is but interrupted silence. Hear the silence of history, of death, the silence of clouds, of snow, the silence of flowers, of all growing things, of trees, mountains, dawn, sunset. Hear the silence of candles burning, the silence of cemeteries, the silence of God, nature, man; of love, grace, sacrifice; the silence of Eucharist. Silence is the special sacrament of God's presence.

The silence of the desert is a source of wisdom, a wisdom developed above all by meditation in solitude upon the mysteries of Christ. The hermit is already "entombed" in a life of eschatological contemplation and solitude. He is a sign of God, destined to remind people of the transitoriness of this world, to present to their gaze an image of the world to come. The man of God seeks God; he seeks by metanoia, inner revolution, solitude to deepen his consciousness, his experience of the Ultimate ground of being and freedom, humility, peace, surrender, transformation and joy, a life of love, of death and resurrection in Christ.

My life is hidden in Christ. "I am quieter inside than even the ocean or the stars." There is enormous hiddenness, solitude, space within each of us. There are also light-years of distance between each of us. We spend most of our time in silence. Significant conversation for the ordinary person averages less than one-half hour a day. We carry within us an immense ocean of silence, silences within silences. Silences exist between us because we do not know what to say, have nothing further to say, or have no place further to go in our relationship.

We have each a "quiet zone." Every sound has its silence. There are people sounds, nature sounds, animal sounds, industry sounds, city sounds — sirens, horns, collisions; sounds of creation, sounds of destruction — building up, tearing down. There is the birth cry of the baby, the cry of a dying person, the sound of laughter and tears. Each day is a new sound, a new interruption, a new silence. Word comes forth from cumulative silence, creates a silence and returns to the silence. The silence of God is the greatest and deepest of all. He sees the truth and waits. Have you found your deepest silence? We live our lives unexplored . . . the depths of our earth, the height of our skies, our off-shore riches.

Holy, Holy, Holy . . . the Eternal Silence of God. How important the Word for him. How important a word from him. We experience his silence more often than we do his words. The silence of his death; the silence of the resurrection; the silence of the Eucharist; the silence of his indwelling in peace, joy, union. In the silence of the Trinity one Word is uttered, one

Spirit poured out, always giving, never being emptied. "We will come to you and make our home within you." Our inmost heart becomes a Holy of Holies and there the Silence of the Father, Son and Spirit speaks their Word, their Love for us. In their silence we are drawn into understanding.

FLOWERS

Yahweh God planted a garden in Eden (Gn 2:8).

The sound of Yahweh God walking in the garden in the cool of the day (Gn 3:8).

He blossoms and he withers, like a flower . . . fleeting like a flower, transient (Jb 14:2).

No longer than a wild flower he lives; one gust of wind and he is gone (Ps 103:15).

I am the rose of Sharon, the lily of the valleys (Sg 2:1).

As a lily among the thistles, so is my love among the maidens (Sg 2:2).

The flowers appear on the earth; the season of glad song is come (Sg 2:12).

She is a garden enclosed, my sister, my promised bride; a garden enclosed, a sealed fountain (Sg 4:12).

Breathe over my garden to spread its sweet smell around. Let my beloved come into his garden, let him taste its rarest fruits (Sg 4:16).

Let the wasteland rejoice and bloom, let it bring forth flowers like the lily; let it rejoice and sing for joy (Is 35:2).

All flesh is grass and its beauty like the wild flower's. The grass withers, the flower fades, but the word of our God remains forever (Is 40:6).

And you shall be like a watered garden (Is 58:11).

For as the earth makes fresh things grow, as a garden makes seeds spring up, so will the Lord Yahweh make both integrity and praise spring up in the sight of the nations (Is 61:11).

Think of the flowers growing in the fields; they never have to work or spin, yet I assure you that not even Solomon in all his regalia was robed like one of these (Mt 6:28).

After he said all this, Jesus left his disciples and crossed the Kedron valley. There was a garden there and he went into it with his disciples (Jn 18:1).

At the place where he had been crucified there was a garden, and in this garden a new tomb in which no one had yet been buried . . . they laid Jesus there (Jn 19:42).

God planted a garden and walked there in the cool of the evening. Jesus often went to pray in a garden. His last prayer before his passion was in a garden. After his death he was buried in a garden. Gardens are for contemplation, prayer. How sensitive was Jesus to the splendor, beauty of flowers, fields. For him, they were the transparent reflection of the glory of his Father.

Flowers are humble, meek, powerless. They are but a sign of something more to come, eventually giving way to the developing fruit. They are but instruments, something to be used by the feet and wings of insects, making pollination possible. Flowers are simply there, yet what magnetic power in their delicateness, fragility, brevity, beauty. To walk in a flower garden is to experience an overwhelming sense of reverence, gratitude for life springing up all about. And the faces of flowers, so many miracles of the Divine Artist, are delightful gifts of his love.

Lovely Flower
Who fashioned thy face
and spreads thy fragrance
upon the fleeting breeze?

Flowers are literally the song, the symphony of the earth. They are the earth breaking forth in joy, exuberance.

In a day, a week, a flower mirrors the whole of a person's life — budding, blooming, fading, dying; spring, summer, fall, winter; child, youth, maturity, old age.

How unresisting are flowers, allowing even the smallest child to pick them. Few other living things yield as easily to children.

Flowers are a sign of love, of devotion, of fidelity — the flowers of the altar. Flowers are for joy, celebrating — the flowers of the family table. Flowers are for gratitude, remembrance— the flowers of the wake, the flowers of the grave.

Cut flowers echo the Paschal mystery, the exquisite beauty given in dying. The sacrifice of flowers — they can be given but once; today is the whole of their life, the only day to give all that they have. The sun expresses its richest, fullest beauty in its setting, its dying. So it is with the flower, its deepest beauty is shown forth in its dying, its total gift. And while it dies, something of its loveliness remains in us forever.

Who brought flowers to Jesus' manger, to Jesus' tomb? — the flowers of Christmas, the flowers of Easter, of Corpus Christi, of Pentecost.

The litany of flowers: wild flowers, mountain flowers, garden flowers, house flowers. We become what we cultivate. We talk to flowers; they talk to us. Flowers teach us; we become indebted to them. They have their own theology as every poet knows. "Flower in the cranny wall, if I knew what you were, root and all, I would know what God and man is."

What is your flower? What flower has picked you? What is your color, your fragrance? What was His flower? His color? His fragrance? All of them! Even me!

Ikebana is the Japanese word for flower arrangement. It means making flowers come to life, a partaking of human life. In the touch of human art, a person becomes alive to flowers in a way in which nature cannot inspire. Flower arrangement is a Zen Buddhist form of meditation, contemplation. It is an act of thanksgiving, enabling one to pray through flowers.

The unplanned beauty of a field can be matter for contemplation as well. One finds an infinite variety of beauty, intricate, unpredictable patterns in the "wild" field never quite without its blossoms. When one flower has lived out the course of its season, another springs up, not to replace, but simply to take its own place in the carefully planned rhythm of the universe.

If there is powerlessness in the flower, there is also strength. Flowers often defy the rules of nature. Some appear in the snow. Others bloom only in the dawn or dusk. Still others appear before leaves have budded. And what could be more wonderful than the desert flower! We are reminded of the familiar quote: "Blossom where you grow." There are spring flowers, spring people: those ahead of their time, fragile, passing, unexpected, full of surprises. There are summer flowers, summer people: the "normal" ones who need love, warmth to grow. There are fall flowers, fall people: strong, straw-like, rich in color, those who take a long time to blossom but who can weather the early frosts that life brings. Lastly, there are winter flowers, winter people: stark, sturdy shells, barren, beautiful structures, those that remain standing in the field after the wind has blown, destined to endure, suffer, still stand when winter has wasted all else so that life may begin again in the spring.

The image of the world full of flowers, a world where an abundance of beauty abounds, is an image of the Kingdom come upon earth. "Justice shall flower in his day, and profound peace till the moon be no more" (Ps 71:7).

BREAD

With sweat on your brow shall you eat your bread (Gn 3:19).

Melchizedek king of Salem brought bread and wine; he was a priest of God Most High (Gn 14:18).

For seven days you must eat unleavened bread . . . The Feast of Unleavened Bread must be kept because it was on that same day I brought you out of Egypt (Ex 12:15).

Then Yahweh said to Moses, "Now I will rain down bread for you from the heavens. Each day the people are to go out and gather the day's portion. I propose to test them in this way to see whether they will follow my law or not. On the sixth day, when they prepare what they have brought in, this will be twice as much as the daily gathering" (Ex 16:4).

In the evening Yahweh will give you meat to eat, in the morning bread to your heart's content (Ex 16:8).

For six days you are to gather it, but on the seventh day —the sabbath—there will be none (Ex 16:26).

The house of Israel named it "manna." It was like coriander seed: it was white and its taste was like that of wafers made with honey (Ex 16:31).

You shall treat him (the priest) as holy, for he offers up the bread of your God. He shall be a holy person to you, because I, Yahweh, am holy, who sanctifies you (Lv 21:8).

The bread on the Golden Table. "You are to take wheaten flour and with it bake twelve loaves . . . Then you must set them in two rows of six on the pure table that stands before Yahweh . . . continually, every sabbath" (Lv 24:5).

He fed you with manna which neither you nor your fathers had known, to make you understand that man does not live on bread alone, but that man lives on everything that comes from the mouth of Yahweh (Dt 8:3).

Come eat of my bread and drink of my wine (Pr 9:5).

If your enemy is hungry, give him bread to eat (Pr 25:21).

A blessing awaits the man who is kindly, since he shares his bread with the poor (Pr 22:9).

Go eat your bread with joy and drink your wine with a glad heart (Qo 9:7).

Cast your bread on the water; at long last you will find it again. (Qo 11:1).

Tell these stones to become bread (Mt 4:3).

Give us this day our daily bread (Mt 6:11).

Then he took the five loaves and the two fish, raised his eyes to heaven and said the blessing. And breaking the loaves he handed them to his disciples who gave them to the crowds (Mt 14:19).

Where could we get enough bread in this deserted place to feed such a crowd? (Mt 15:33).

On the first day of unleavened bread, when the Passover lamb was sacrificed, his disciples said to him, "Where do you want us to go and make the preparations for you to eat the Passover?" (Mk 14:12).

Then he took some bread and when he had given thanks, broke it and gave it to them, saying, "This is my body which will be given for you; do this as a memorial of me" (Lk 22:19).

Then they told their story of what had happened on the road and how they had recognized him at the breaking of the bread (Lk 24:35).

I tell you most solemnly it was not Moses who gave you bread from heaven, it is my Father who gives you the bread from heaven, the true bread: for the bread of God is that which comes down from heaven and gives life to the world (Jn 6:32).

"Sir," they said, "give us that bread always." Jesus answered, "I am the bread of life. He who comes to me will never be hungry" (Jn 6:34).

I am the bread of life. Your fathers ate the manna in the desert and they are dead; but this is the bread that comes down from heaven. Anyone who eats this bread will live forever. And the bread that I shall give is my flesh for the life of the world (Jn 6:48).

Someone who has eaten bread with me betrays me (Jn 13:18).

As soon as they came ashore they saw that there was

some bread there, and a charcoal fire with fish cooking on it (Jn 21:9).

These remained faithful to the teaching of the apostles, to the brotherhood, to the breaking of the bread and to the prayers (Ac 2:42).

Met in their houses for the breaking of the bread (Ac 2:47).

On the first day of the week we met to break bread (Ac 20:7).

Then Paul went back upstairs where he broke bread and ate and carried on talking till he left at daybreak (Ac 20:11).

With these words he took some bread, gave thanks to God in front of them all, broke it and began to eat (Ac 27:35).

The bread that we break is a communion with the body of Christ. The fact that there is only one loaf means that, though there are many of us, we form a single body because we all have a share in this one loaf (1 Co 10:17).

Until the Lord comes, therefore, every time you eat this bread and drink this cup, you are proclaiming his death, and so anyone who eats the bread or drinks the cup of the Lord unworthily will be behaving unworthily toward the body and blood of the Lord (1 Co 11:26).

Matthew tells us that Jesus "fasted for forty days and forty nights, after which he was very hungry." This is Matthew's description of Jesus as he begins his public life. In the final chapter of Luke's Gospel the last question of Jesus which Luke records is, "Have you anything here to eat?" (Lk 24:42). How impressive this human hunger of Jesus. How many of us seem to have inherited his appetite! Luke continues in his Gospel that "they offered him a piece of grilled fish, which he took and ate before their eyes." I think that Jesus might have preferred fresh bread! He was born in Bethlehem, the house of bread. And how meaningful bread must have been to Jesus as he took it into his hands each day. What anticipated joy must have welled up within him as he reflected that someday all bread would become holy because he had transformed it into his body to be given for us. How concerned he was to feed the multitudes with the bread of the earth. How much more concerned was he that we eat the bread that comes down from heaven!

Bread is indeed the staff of life, the universal food for all mankind, for each person at every stage of life. Nature does not produce bread directly. The first mention of bread in Scripture is with reference to "the sweat of the brow." Bread is a creation of man, a distinctively human product. Where you find bread, you find man. How many millennia of evolution took place in the making of bread. Even today it is no simple feat to make bread. And the thousand different forms it can take. Every culture, nationality has its own distinctive bread. And how much of a nationality is reflected in its bread alone. In the history of the world, how important is bread. How many wars have been fought, how many people have died because there was not enough bread. Even today, how universal the cry, "They have no bread." How much anxiety in cities and families when the *breadwinner* has no work and people are forced to wait in never-ending *bread*-lines.

Bread is the work of human hands, the basic manual labor. We cannot feed ourselves from within our own imagination, thoughts or ideas. The mind depends upon bread. It must come from outside ourselves. It always comes as total gift. It is always a blessing, leading us to prayer, to gratitude, to thanksgiving, to Eucharist. We can almost live on bread alone. Without it, we will die, but bread alone is not enough.

> It is the spirit that gives life,
> the flesh has nothing to offer.
> The words I have spoken to you are spirit and they are life (Jn 6:63).
>
> I am the living bread that has come down from heaven. Anyone who eats this bread will live forever.

Jesus is the Breadwinner; the Eucharist is the breadline which leads us into life everlasting.

WINE

> Noah, a tiller of the soil, was the first to plant the vine. He drank some of the wine and was drunk (Gn 9:20).
>
> Melchizedek, king of Salem, brought bread and wine. He was a priest of God Most High (Gn 14:19).
>
> The libation of strong wine for Yahweh must be poured out in the sanctuary (No 28:7).
>
> Wine which cheers the heart of gods and men (Jg 9:13).
>
> The wine is for drinking by those who grow weary in the wilderness (2 S 16:3).
>
> You have allowed your people to suffer, to drink a wine that makes us reel (Ps 60:3).
>
> Then like a sleeper, like a hero fighting-mad with wine, the Lord woke up to strike his enemies on the rump, and put them to everlasting shame (Ps 78:65).
>
> Wine to make them cheerful (Ps 104:15).
>
> What return can I make to Yahweh for all his goodness to me? I will offer (wine) libations to my saviour, invoking the name of Yahweh (Ps 116:13).
>
> For those who linger over wine too long ever on the lookout for the well-blended wine. Never relish how red it is, this wine, how sparkling in the cup, how smooth its flow. In the end its bite is like a serpent's, its sting as sharp as an adder's (Pr 23:30).
>
> Procure strong drink for a man about to perish, wine for the heart that is full of bitterness. Let him drink and forget his misfortune and remember his misery no more (Pr 31:6).
>
> But meals are made for laughter. Wine gives joy to life (Qo 10:19).

Your love is more delightful than wine . . . We shall praise your love above wine (Sg 1:2 & 4).

How delicious is your love, more delicious than wine (Sg 4:10).

I drink my wine and my milk. Eat, friends, and drink, drink deep, my dearest friends (Sg 5:1).

Your speaking, superlative wine. Wine flowing straight to my Beloved (Sg 7:9).

No, they put new wine into fresh skins and both are preserved (Mt 9:17).

They offered him wine mixed with myrrh, but he refused it (Mk 15:23).

They have no wine . . . fill the jars with water . . . and it turned into wine . . . but you have kept the best wine till now. (Jn 2:4).

The Son of Man comes, eating and drinking (Lk 7:34).

Then he took a cup, and when he had returned thanks he gave it to them. "Drink all of you from this," he said, "for this is my blood, the blood of the covenant, which is to be poured out for many for the forgiveness of sins. From now on I tell you, I shall not drink wine until the day I drink the new wine with you in the kingdom of my father" (Mt 26:27).

I am the true vine, and my Father is the vinedresser. You are the branches. Whoever remains in me, with me in him, bears fruit in plenty; for cut off from me you can do nothing. So that my own joy may be in you and your joy be complete I commissioned you to go out and to bear fruit, fruit that will last (Jn 15).

"They have been drinking too much new wine," they said (Ac 2:13).

You should give up drinking only water and have a little wine for the sake of your digestion (1 Tm 5:23).

The first mention of wine in Scripture is in Genesis. Noah was the first to plant the vine. He drank some of the wine and was drunk. The second mention of wine is also in Genesis. "Melchizedek, king of Salem, brought bread and wine; he was a priest of God Most High." Such is the story of wine from the beginning of time even down to our own day. "God saw all that he had made, and indeed it was very good." Yet in man's hands a good thing can become either a curse or a blessing, a lifting up or a throwing down.

Wine is the cup of desolation or the cup of joy. Wine is the drink of weddings and funerals. Wine cheers the heart of God and man. God loves to see us happy. Wine is the comfort of the poor. Wine is a celebration, the language of love, of joy.

How wonderful it is that Jesus came "eating and drinking," that Mary's first words at the beginning of his public life were, "They have no wine."

Jesus is the great wine-maker, the brother of all Cellar Masters. He declared himself the true vine into which we are grafted. His Spirit is new wine in us. He commands us to take his cup and to drink deeply the wine turned blood which proclaims his death and resurrection, which consoles us until he comes again.

And he waits for us in the Kingdom of his Father where we will drink the new wine with him. Until that day, we are to be his wine, his joy, his resurrection.

JOB

At this my own heart quakes,
    and leaps from its place.
Listen, oh listen, to the blast of his voice
    and the sound that blares from his mouth.
He hurls his lightning below the span of heaven,
    it strikes to the very ends of the earth.
After it comes the roar of his voice,
    the peal of God's majestic thunder.

He does not check his thunderbolts
until his voice resounds no more.
No doubt of it, but God reveals wonders,
and does great deeds that we cannot understand.
When he says to the snow, 'Fall on the earth'
or tells the rain to pour down in torrents,
he brings all men's strivings to a standstill
so that each must acknowledge his hand at
work.
All the beasts go back to their dens,
taking shelter in their lairs.
The storm wind comes from the Mansion of the
South,
and the north winds usher in the cold.
God breathes, and the ice is there,
the surface of the waters freezes over.
He weighs the clouds down with moisture,
and the storm clouds radiate his lightning.
He himself guides their wheeling motion,
directing all their seasonal changes:
they carry out his orders to the letter
all over his inhabited world.
Whether for punishing earth's peoples
or for a work of mercy, he dispatches them.
Listen to all this, Job: no backsliding now!
Can you tell how God controls them
or how his clouds make the lightning flash?
Can you tell how he holds the clouds in balance:
a miracle of consummate skill?
When your clothes are hot to your body
and the earth lies still under the south wind,
can you help him to spread the vault of heaven,
or temper that mirror of cast metal?
Tell me what to say to him:

Can my words carry weight with him?
   Do man's commands reach his ears?
There are times when the light vanishes
   behind darkening clouds;
then comes the wind, sweeping them away,
   and brightness spreads from the north.
God is clothed in fearful splendor:
   he, Shaddai, is far beyond our reach.
Supreme in power, in equity,
   excelling in justice, yet no oppressor —
no wonder that men fear him,
   and thoughtful men hold him in awe.

LATE HAVE I LOVED YOU

Late have I loved You
   O beauty ever ancient, ever new!
Late have I loved You
   And behold,
You were within; and I without,
   and without I sought You.
And deformed I ran after these forms
   of beauty You have made.
You were with me
   And I was not with You.
Those things held me back from You,
   things whose only being
   was to be in You.
You called; You cried;
   and You broke through my deafness.
You flashed; You shone;
   and you chased away my blindness.
You became fragrant;
   and I inhaled and sighed for You.
I tasted
   and now hunger and thirst
   for You.
You touched me;
   and I burned for Your embrace.

—Prayer of St. Augustine

59

CHILDREN

God blessed them, saying to them, "Be fruitful, multiply, fill the earth" (Gn 1:28).

Then taking him outside, he said, "Look up to heaven and count the stars if you can. Such will be your descendants," he told him (Gn 15:6).

How Yahweh carried you, as a man carries his child, all along the road you travel on the way to this place (Dt 1:31).

Sons are a bounty from Yahweh, he rewards with descendants (Ps 127:3).

Your wife a fruitful vine on the inner walls of your house, your sons around your table like shoots 'round an olive tree (Ps 128:3).

Enough for me to keep my soul tranquil and quiet like a child in its mother's arms, as content as a child that has been weaned (Ps 131:2).

When Israel was a child I loved him and I called my son out of Egypt . . . I myself taught Ephraim to walk, I took them in my arms; yet they have not understood that I was the one looking after them. I was like someone who lifts an infant close against his cheek; stooping down to him I gave him his food (Ho 11:1).

And a little child shall lead them (Is 11:6).

The virgin will conceive and give birth to a son and they will call him Immanuel (Is 7:14; Mt 1:33).

In Bethlehem and its surrounding districts he had all the male children killed who were two years old or under . . .

A voice was heard in Ramah,
sobbing and loudly lamenting:
it was Rachel weeping for her children
refusing to be comforted
because they were no more (Mt 3:16; Jr 31:15).

Blessed are the peacemakers, they shall be called children of God (Mt 5:10).

Love your enemies and pray for those who persecute you; in this way you will be children of your Father in Heaven (Mt 5:44).

They are like children shouting to each other as they sit in the market place (Mt 11:16).

The good seed is the children of the kingdom (Mt 13:38).

Anyone who welcomes a little child like this in my name welcomes me (Mt 18:5).

See that you never despise any of these little ones, for I tell you that their angels in heaven are continually in the presence of my Father in heaven (Mt 18:10).

Who is the greatest in the kingdom of heaven? So he called a little child to him and set the child in front of them. Then he said, "I tell you solemnly, unless you change and become like little children you will never enter the kingdom of heaven. And so, the one who makes himself as little as this child is the greatest in the kingdom of heaven" (Mt 19:1).

People brought little children to him for him to lay his hands on them and say a prayer (Mt 19:13).

At the sight of the wonderful things he did and of the children shouting, "Hosanna to the son of David" in the temple, the chief priests and scribes were indignant. "Do you hear what they are saying?" "Yes," Jesus answered, "have you never read this:

By the mouths of children, babes in arms, you have made sure of praise?" (Mt 21:16).

How often have I longed to gather your children, as a hen gathers her chicks under her wings (Mt 23:38).

And anyone who welcomes me, welcomes not me but the one who sent me (Mk 9:37).

The disciples turned them away, but when Jesus saw this he was indignant and said to them, "Let the little children come to me, do not stop them; for it is to such as these that the kingdom of heaven belongs. I tell you solemnly, anyone who does not welcome the kingdom of God like a little child will never enter it." Then he put his arms around them, laid his hands on them and gave them his blessing (Mk 10:13).

Now as soon as Elizabeth heard Mary's greeting, the child leaped in her womb and Elizabeth was filled with the Holy Spirit (Lk 1:41).

And found Mary and Joseph, and the baby lying in the manger (Lk 2:16).

You see this child: he is destined for the fall and for the rising of many in Israel (Lk 2:34).

For the children of this world are more astute in dealing with their own kind than are the children of light (Lk 16:8).

Daughters of Jerusalem, do not weep for me, weep rather for yourselves and for your children (Lk 23:28).

While you still have the light believe in the light and you will become sons of light (Jn 12:36).

My little children, I shall not be with you much longer (Jn 13:33).

The Spirit himself and our spirit bear united witness that we are children of God. And if we are children we are heirs as well: heirs of God and co-heirs with Christ, sharing his sufferings so as to share his glory (Rm 8:16).

To enjoy the glorious freedom of the children of God (Rm 8:21).

When I was a child, I used to talk like a child, and think like a child and argue like a child but now I am a man, all childish ways are put behind me (1 Co 13:11).

I speak as if to children of mine (2 Co 6:13).

And you are, all of you, sons of God through faith in Christ Jesus (Ga 3:26).

My children! I must go through the pain of giving birth to you all over again, until Christ is formed in you (Ga 4:19).

To live through love in his presence, determining that we should be his adopted children (Ep 1:5).

Try then to imitate God, as children of his that he loves (Ep 5:1).

Live in Christ, then, my children (1 Jn 2:28).

Think of the love that the Father has lavished on us by letting us be called God's children (1 Jn 3:1).

Now a great sign appeared in heaven: a woman, adorned with the sun, standing on the moon, and with twelve stars on her head for a crown. She was pregnant, and in labor, crying aloud in the pangs of childbirth (Rv 12:1).

We are already beyond childhood when we begin to recognize children, yet we never let go of our lost childhood. Every year of our childhood remains within us and our delight with little children is in having them discover the little child in us.

Children are little people and we are continually amazed at their various sizes, shapes, forms. Some people are bird watchers; but all people are child watchers. Children give birth to adults time and again. How a child can lead us, free us, unite us! How much peace, joy, hope a child can bring to a street, a room, a bus, a plane.

To walk with a child is to learn how to walk all over again. It is to see with new eyes, to hear with new ears, to touch with new hands. Children are the first blessing uttered by God in creation. And every child is a promise, a guarantee that God has not yet given up on the world.

> The joy of children's eyes
>   the innocence of their touch
>   their totality of faith
>   the unrestraint of their love!

The world of a child is today, the immediate environment, what I see, touch, smell, taste. Knowledge, the history of good and evil have not yet appeared. There exists unlimited possibility for goodness or its opposite. It is the age of unpremeditation; everything is total experience. Reflection, understanding are but beginning.

What would our life be like without little children? What would happen to us without Christmas? "Jesus was a baby!" He has lived every year of our childhood. How central is his theme, "Unless you become like little children." "A little child shall lead them." The more we discover the Father, Abba, the more we can become little children.

FAMILY...FRIENDS

Yahweh would speak to Moses face to face as a man speaks with his friend (Ex 33:11).

The wife you cherish, or the friend with whom you share your life . . . (Dt 13:6).

O Jonathan, in your death I am stricken. I am desolate for you, my brother. Very dear to me you were. Your love was more wonderful than the love of a woman (2 S 1:26).

Tobit said: What family and what tribe do you belong to? (Tb 5:15).

Tobit left the house to set out and kissed his father and mother (Tb 5:22).

Yahweh restored Job's fortunes because he had prayed for his friends (Jb 42:10).

Your wife: A fruitful vine, on the inner walls of your house. Your sons: around your table, like shoots around an olive tree (Ps 128:3).

You are all brothers. How good. How delightful it is for all to live together like brothers (Ps 133:1).

A friend is a friend at all times. It is for adversity that a brother is born (Pr 17:17).

There are friends that lead one to ruin, others are closer than a brother (Pr 18:24).

Do not abandon friend or father's friend. Better a friend near than a brother far away (Pr 27:10).

Iron is made finer with iron. A man is refined by contact with his friend (Pr 27:17).

Listen to the Word of Yahweh, house of Jacob and all you families of the House of Israel (Jr 2:4).

I will be the God of all the families of Israel. They shall be my people (Jr 21:1).

A friend of tax collectors and sinners (Mt 11:19).

Anyone who does the will of my Father in heaven, he is my brother, and sister and mother (Mt 12:50).

Bethany — home of Jesus' friends.

> *With that he left them and went out of the city to Bethany where he spent the night (Mt 21:17).*

> *Jesus was at Bethany in the house of Simon the leper, when a woman came to him with an alabaster jar of ointment (Mt 26:6).*

My friend, do what you are here for (Mt 26:50).

Who are my Mother and my Brother? Anyone who does the will of God, that person is my brother and sister and mother (Mk 3:34-5).

He was of the house and family of David (Lk 2:4).

When they had done everything the Law of the Lord required they went back to Galilee, to their own town of Nazareth. Meanwhile the child grew to maturity, and he was filled with wisdom: and God's favor was with him (Lk 2:39).

He then went down with them and came to Nazareth and lived under their authority. His Mother stored up all these things in her heart. And Jesus increased in wisdom, in stature, and in favor with God and men (Lk 2:51).

There was a wedding at Cana in Galilee . . . and Jesus and his disciples had also been invited . . . This was the first of the signs given by Jesus . . . He let his glory be seen (Jn 3).

There was a man named Lazarus who lived in the village of Bethany with the two sisters, Mary and Martha (Jn 11:1).

And Jesus wept. See how he loved him (Jn 11:36).

Six days before the Passover, Jesus went to Bethany, where Lazarus was . . . They gave a dinner for him there: Martha waited on them . . . Mary anointed the feet of Jesus (Jn 12:1).

A man can have no greater love than to lay down his life for his friends. You are my friends, if you do what I command you. I shall not call you servants any more . . . I call you friends, because I have made known to you everything I have learned from my Father (Jn 15:13).

This is your mother. And from that moment the disciple made a place for her in his home (Jn 19:27).

He had asked his relatives and close friends to be there (Ac 10:24).

And Julius was considerate enough to allow Paul to go to his friends to be looked after (Ac 27:3).

Paul's lists of friends and co-workers: Greetings from your friends; greet each of our friends by name.

This then is what I pray, kneeling before the Father, from whom every family whether spiritual or material takes its name (Ep 3:14).

Husbands should love their wives just as Christ loved the Church and sacrificed himself for her to make her holy . . . For this reason a man must leave his father and *mother and be joined to his wife, and the two will become one body . . . Children, be obedient to your parents in the Lord . . . Honor your father and mother . . . and you will prosper and have a long life in the land (Ep 5:25).*

And that is why Moses is called: Friend of God (Jm 2:23).

I have a family! I am a home and family. I share the same father and mother. I have brothers and sisters. Together we go back through common ancestry to a common land. We began a long time ago. The holy, the sinful, the love, the violence, the greatness, the shame that is our family. Imagine! All the brothers and sisters we might have had!

Family is a way of growing up together, a way of mutual discovery, exploration, remembrance. Family is totality of life together, living in one another's lives: their laughter, my laughter; their tears, my tears. Our first experience of serving one another, playing, working, affection, tenderness, misunderstanding, hurt, happen in the family. Family is our earliest experience of eating together with others. Before we left home we had probably at least 15,000 meals together. Our first entertainment was found at home — toys, cards, games. Our first celebrations were in the family — birthdays, picnics, summer outings. First Communion, Confirmation, weddings, funerals, baptisms, were occasions for family gatherings. The family went visiting together, streetcar rides across the city to visit the relatives, first cousins, aunts, uncles, neighbors. The grown-ups talked but the children were bashful and eventually slipped away to delight and play with one another in the backyard, alley, on bicycles, scooters, wagons. Every family had its own special times: Sunday afternoon walks, church together, praying at meals, rosary, night prayer. Who of us can forget Sunday morning breakfast, funny papers, having special friends over, rainy days, days sick in bed? We each carry the memory of going for a walk down the avenue, walking with Dad through the park, riding the streetcar downtown to shop and be fitted for school; going grocery shopping with Mother — the meat market, bakery, going down to Frenchies', the corner candy store with its speciality of gingerbread and mint leaves. Growing up meant going across the street, playing with the kids in the neighborhood, games of tag and hide-go-seek.

Bedtime was a family affair: waiting one's turn for the bathroom or sneaking in before someone else did; darkness and cold sheets; bedtime stories; pretending to be asleep; talking in bed at night, fooling around and making noises till Mom or Dad had to come and spank everyone; sneaking down on the landing to listen in on the conversation of the company or the men playing cards.

We have so many memories of Thanksgiving, Christmas, New Year's, Easter: eating in the dining room instead of the kitchen; midnight Mass, choir, being an altar boy; listening to the horns and whistles bring in the New Year. Perhaps we still smell the Christmas tree, feel the excitement of decorating, shopping, playing in the snow. Our first experiences of Lent, Easter, were in the family: stations of the cross, holy week, Easter baskets, coloring eggs.

Home, family, is a gift. Every day of the week made us into a family: Saturday — shopping, confession, play, Saturday night baths, shoe polish; Sunday afternoon devotions for the sick in the parish at 2:30; Monday—wash day; Tuesday — ironing and at 7:30 Perpetual Help Devotions; Wednesday — housecleaning; Holy Hour on Thursday from 7:00-8:00.

There were so many ways of becoming a family—doing homework on the dining room table, being called home for dinner, coming in when the street lights went on; Dad coming home from work, crossing the street to meet him, excitement over the surprise for us in his lunch pail. Becoming a family happened in the annual work of cutting grass, raking leaves, shoveling snow, sweeping the sidewalk; cutting hedges, weeding the garden, whitewashing the basement, cleaning the cupboards, taking out and storing the storm windows, putting up the screens.

Tobit asked: What family and what tribe do you belong to? (Tb 5:15). There are certain cumulative experiences which make a family: listening to favorite radio programs, sharing comic books, having a ton of coal delivered in the street and wheelbarrowing it into the coal bin; finding discarded lumber, wood, cutting it up for winter; learning to take care of the coal furnace in the basement, starting the fire, checking the chimney, cleaning the furnace each year, dismantling the whole furnace, cleaning the soot out of the pipes with wire brushes.

Family will always be the special place of beginning: starting to work, getting a paper route, working in the dime store; going off to high school; taking more time with friends than with family. Certain friends begin to become more a part of the family. A wonderful new stage of family begins with the first marriage, the birth of the second generation.

Tobit kissed his mother and father, left the house, set out (Tb 3:22). Family is the origin of a new, mysterious affinity, at-homeness with another, the coming together of two histories, two different life experiences. A new door is opened into one another, a door neither was aware of before. "You are different from me, but we were born involved in each other." The discovery of another self is the discovery of oneself. It is learning to articulate, to own what one is, so as to share it with another.

In the building up, the deepening of relationships, how far can we go? We each have intuitive ways of gardening a friendship, sharing life and growth. We cannot return to our parents what they have given us; we can only pass it on. There is a certain point when friends become brothers and sisters, and when brothers and sisters become friends, the point when we have shared as much time living away from the family as we have lived within the family. New friendships begin, old friendships last — like spring flowers and like old maple trees. Some friends disappear, die. Certain friendships are ruptured, broken, and the pain still lingers. We all live in outer and inner circles; we carry hidden questions like: "Is there any more love in me? Has it reached its depth and height? Am I all mined out? Who will lead me?" "Every friendship enriches one's capacity for friendship and enriches all previous friendships. One's capacity is stretched until he wonders how many can fit around his table . . . We have the capacity for God, therefore, we have the capacity in some way for the four billion other persons who breathe this planet's air with us."

Family is sacrament. Jesus had a family: father, mother, cousins, relatives, neighbors. He was of the house and family of David (Lk 2:4). He has made all of us members of his family. How many families in the Mystical Body! The family of Father, Son and Holy Spirit is the origin of every family. We are adopted into the Holy Family by the blood of Jesus, by love. We are members of the family by blood, by shared life, joy, sorrow, celebration. We are made into a family by common spirit, affection, breath, joy. In Christ, all of us are a family of friends, of grace. How can we receive the holiness, the grace of our family, and tend with care our family skeleton, our family saints, our family wisdom and proverbs, the hidden life, love, joy, peace, intimate community, mystery of our family?

How many families do we know? In how many families do we find ourselves? Who is our heritage, our genealogy; who are our ancestors, our clustering clan? We have each an almost unlimited capacity for family, an unlimited experience of sharing, enjoying one another, remembering, celebrating. We are all brothers and sisters. We are always evangelizing, making others members of our family, making them members of His family. The cumulative presence of our family enables us to pray together: "Our Father . . ."

PEOPLE

Ah! What is man that you should spare a thought for him, the son of man that you should care for him? Yet you have made him little less than a god. You have crowned him with glory and splendor (Ps 8:4).

Wine to make them cheerful, oil to make them happy, and bread to make them strong (Ps 104:15).

. . . delighting to be with the sons of men (Pr 8:31).

I feel sorry for all these people; they have been with me for three days now and have nothing to eat (Mt 15:32).

Jesus felt compassion for them and touched their eyes and immediately their sight returned and they followed him (Mt 20:34).

If you want to, he said, you can cure me. Feeling compassion for him Jesus stretched out his hand and touched him. Of course I want to! he said. Be cured! (Mk 1:40).

And all the people came to him and he taught them (Mk 2:13).

Great numbers who had heard of all he was doing came to him (Mk 3:8).

Then the woman came forward, frightened and trembling . . . my daughter, he said, your faith has restored you to health, go in peace and be free from your complaint (Mk 5:33).

If anyone gives you a cup of water to drink . . . (Mk 9:41).

Jesus looked steadily at him and loved him (Mk 10:21).

And he sat down opposite the treasury and watched the people putting money into the treasury (Mk 12:41).

And at the hour of incense a whole multitude was outside praying (Lk 1:10).

And eveyone in the crowd was trying to touch him because power came out of him that cured them all (Lk 6:19).

When the Lord saw her he felt compassion for her. Do not cry, he said . . . and the dead man sat up and began to talk and Jesus gave him to his mother (Lk 7:13).

When Jesus reached the spot he looked up and spoke to him: Zacchaeus, come down. Hurry, because I must stay at your house today (Lk 19:5).

Daughters of Jerusalem, do not weep for me, weep rather for yourselves and for your children (Lk 23:28).

Father, forgive them. They do not know what they are doing (Lk 23:34).

Indeed I promise you, he replied, today you will be with me in paradise (Lk 23:43).

When a Samaritan woman came to draw water, Jesus said to her: Give me to drink (Jn 4:7).

Centurion: When Jesus heard these words he was astonished at him and, turning around, said to the crowd following him: I tell you, not even in Israel have I found faith like this (Jn 7:9).

The multitude that believed were united, heart and soul (Ac 4:32).

After this I saw before me a huge crowd which no one could count from every nation and race, people and tongue (Rv 7:9).

The deepest contemplation next to God is another person. You are little less than the angels, crown of creation, image of God. What is man that you are mindful of him? Every person is a mystery hidden from all eternity. O sacrament most holy . . . all praise and all thanksgiving be every moment thine! Each person is image of God, a revelation, a transfiguration, a waiting for him to manifest himself.

The most beautiful, fascinating creature in all the world is another person — the face, smile, eyes, vibration, walk, voice. In a single face, in a few round inches there is incredible variety. Every face is another window of the world, transparent or opaque, in light or darkness. Every face is a new world, a new adventure which expands or contracts my world. But while I am peopled by many faces, touched by many eyes, listened to by many ears, I relate face-to-face with few. Eyes are quick. They can see a hundred thousand people in a glance. In contrast, ears are slow, exclusive. I can hear but one person at a time.

We are each aware of crowds of people: meeting people, greeting them, welcoming them, saying hello, saying goodbye. We come to see more and more people; we come to know fewer and fewer. How many anonymous people in our lives? While each is a member of my family, all are somehow strangers. Each person is a stranger in a strange land. I experience the anonymity of crowded beach, busy airport. There is the pressure of greater anonymity, knowing no one's name, no one knowing my name. There is little room left in me for them; there is little room left in them for me. I know fewer and fewer; I am known less and less. But while there is the pressure of passing so many people, each passing can be a loving, a touching, a praying, a blessing with a smile, a thanksgiving. Every person I pass or meet receives from me and imparts to me a blessing.

What must have been the anguish of the heart of Christ, loving so many so deeply, preaching to the multitudes, feeding them with bread yet remaining only on the edge of their lives. How did Jesus handle the nameless crowd?

How few people we know by name. How few we know in their inmost heart. We are all people-watchers. In a glance we see multitudes. In a simple look we see more people in a stadium, a theater, shopping center than we will meet in our lifetime. Each person is a gift, joy, grace, sacrament of his presence. Each person is a message, a ministry, an invitation. We are all the Mystical Body, the communion of saints, communion of sinners. We are indebted to all of mankind, to all of its history — to the anonymous hands which have built this building or my home, have made the clothes I wear, the food I eat, the furnishings of my room, the car I drive and the roads I travel. There is an interconnectedness between all of our lives, between all of the people who have built my city, provided my water, heat, electricity, phone, mail, and all the other anonymous services I enjoy.

People are a daily act of thanksgiving. All the media people, newspaper, movies, TV, we know by name and face whom we will never meet, whose places we will never visit. There are many people we have met but once whose names we have forgotten, many upon whom we have looked with love but with whom we could not share that love. There are people who have disappeared out of our lives by death, moving away, drifting. In the long, rapid march of time there are new people coming into our lives, others fading away. What communion, wholeness happens when we are thankful, willing good for others, when we are benefactor, when we leave something, do something with our lives for others.

Each person who knows my name has a unique way of saying it, calling me, seeing me, mirroring me, hearing me. We say each person's name as it has never been said before. We are an unknown self to one another, creating each other, stretching, contracting, praising. The expression of praise makes a community. The prayer most pleasing to God is our praise of one another. "Let them cultivate the art of praise in dealing with one another and with those they serve. Let them freely and sincerely express their esteem for one another, their gratitude and respect. Let them not withhold from one another, and especially from their sister, what the heart tells them should be hers."

The greatest charism is loving, because only love reveals the truth within another person and mirrors this grace to them. Our greatest achievement is not in art or work but in human friendship, being with, to, and for others. Love is our greatest power. It depends not on culture, education, talent, skill but on our human heart. Each person has a unique love, a unique life shared, known by no one else. Each has a truth, a secret, a wish, a prayer.

Over and again we are learning to celebrate one another, learning to celebrate ourselves. And if we do not know how, people will show us. Each day is a birthday! "What I like about you . . ." is an attitude worthy of every person. The truest celebration is to see each other through another's eyes, to discover the beautiful sensitivity in one another, to discover more of one another's grace. One of the most special of virtues is that of admiration. We do not admire ourselves enough, believe in ourselves enough. In the fraternal huddle, in home entertainment, in the charism of secret service, how much we can learn from each other, how much we can grow. There is no one person who can fully appreciate me; each person uncovers but one of the colors of my rainbow. It takes a whole community to discover the rainbow. How much we do not see, do not appreciate in one another. Yet, we have each a unique, original appreciation of the other. We have each a unique, secret, insight. We need more embarrassing moments to enjoy the celebration of one another. How long it takes to know another person; how long to let myself be known!

JOY

But joy for all who take shelter in you, endless shouts of joy (Ps 5:11).

In your presence is fullness of joy and at your right hand everlasting pleasures (Ps 16:11).

In the morning shouts of joy (Ps 30:5).

The holy mountain, beautiful where it rises, joy of the whole world (Ps 48:1).

Instill some joy and gladness into me . . . Be my Savior again, renew my joy (Ps 51:8).

Those that sow in tears shall reap in joy (Ps 126:5).

I was by his side, a master craftsman, delighting him day by day, ever at play in his presence, at play everywhere in his world, delighting to be with the sons of men (Pr 8:30).

So long as God keeps his heart occupied with joy (Qo 5:19).

Go, eat your bread with joy and drink your wine with a glad heart (Qo 9:7).

I will make them joyful in my house of prayer (Is 56:7).

Come to me, all you who labor and are overburdened, and I will give you rest. Shoulder my yoke and learn from me, for I am gentle and humble in heart, and you will find rest for your souls (Mt 11:28).

For the moment your greeting reached my ears, the child in my womb leaped for joy (Lk 1:44).

Listen, I bring you news of great joy (Lk 2:10).

Rejoice when that day comes and dance for joy (Lk 6:23)

There will be more joy in heaven over one repentant sinner than over ninety-nine virtuous men who have no need for repentance (Lk 15:7).

He showed them his hands and feet. Their joy was so great that they could not believe it (Lk 24:41).

They worshipped him and then went back to Jerusalem full of joy (Lk 24:53).

And yet the bridegroom's friend who stands there and listens, is glad when he hears the bridegroom's voice. This same joy I feel and now it is complete (Jn 3:29).

I have told you this so that my own joy may be in you and your joy be complete (Jn 15:11).

Your sorrow will turn to joy . . . (Jn 16:20).

You are sad now, but I shall see you again and your hearts will be full of joy and that joy no one shall take from you (Jn 16:22).

Ask and you will receive and so your joy will be complete (Jn 16:24).

While still in the world I say these things to share my joy with them to the full (Jn 17:13).

The disciples were filled with joy and the Holy Spirit (Ac 13:49).

May the God of hope bring you such joy and peace in your faith that the power of the Holy Spirit will remove all bounds to hope (Rm 15:13).

I am sure you all know that I could never be happy unless you were (2 Co 2:4).

I am so proud of you that in all our trouble I am filled with consolation and my joy is overflowing (2 Co 7:4)

What the Spirit brings is very different: love, joy, peace (Ga 5:22).

And every time I pray for all of you, I pray with joy (Ph 1:3).

And help you to progress in the faith and even increase your joy in it (Ph 1:26).

And then if my blood has to be shed as part of your own sacrifice and offering — which is your faith — I shall still be happy and rejoice with all of you and you must be just as happy and rejoice with me (Ph 2:18).

I miss you very much, dear friends; you are my joy and my crown (Ph 4:1).

And it was with the joy of the Holy Spirit that you took to the Gospel, in spite of the great opposition all around you (1 Th 1:6).

What do you think is our pride and joy? You are; and you will be the crown of which we shall be proudest in the presence of our Lord Jesus when he comes; you are our pride and our joy (1 Th 2:19).

How can we thank God enough for you, for all the joy we feel before our God on your account? (1 Th 3:9).

I remember your tears and long to see you again to complete my joy (2 Tm 1:4).

Well then, brother, I am counting on you, in the Lord, put new joy (heart) into me, in Christ (Phm 1:20).

For the sake of the joy that was still in the future, he endured the cross (Heb 12:2).

You will always have your trials but, when they come, try to treat them as a joy (Jm 1:2).

You did not see him, yet you love him; and still without seeing him, you are already filled with a joy so glorious that it cannot be described (1 P 1:8).

You should be glad, because it means that you are called to share Christ's sufferings. One day, when he shows himself in full splendor to men, you will be filled with the most tremendous joy (1 P 4:13).

We are writing this to make our own joy complete (1 Jn 1:4).

I hope instead to visit you and talk to you personally, so that our joy may be complete (2 Jn 12).

It is always my greatest joy to hear that my children are living according to the truth (3 Jn 4).

To the poor he proclaimed the good news of salvation . . . and to those in sorrow joy.

"Listen, I bring you news of great joy." Joy is the distinctive mark of a Christian: The Good News in joy. Perhaps a better, more essential translation of our theological word "grace" is "joy." Joy is the transparency of grace, the overflow of his presence into us, into the lives of others. Joy is a gift; at the same time, it is for every Christian a responsibility. If joy is a gift, then we must ask for it, seek it, knock on its door until it is opened to us.

Joy is a flame; it cannot exist of itself; it must be fueled, fed.

Joy, like happiness, does not exist in itself; it is a sign, an effect, a consequence of someone's presence. Joy is the gift, the fruit of the Holy Spirit.

Because it is "through Him all things came to be, not one thing had its being but through Him. All that came to be had life in Him" (Jn 1:3).

There is the guilt of joy. What right do I have to be happy when the rest of the world is in anguish? "Our life, our sweetness and our hope."

There is the joy of the poor, the anawim who have nothing but Jesus. Their poverty is the condition, the predisposition for Gospel and they have been led there by the Spirit. He leads us to this kind of poverty; he leads us to use all that we have for the poor.

Joy is spiritual. The pleasure society is not the joyful society, the happy society. Witness the malaise of boredom, depression, sadness. Joy comes from another source.

Everything is joy, everything comes from him, is blessed, is for us. The Sacrament of creation.

He has made us for joy. Everything has been touched by him, everything is a gift from him. We cannot escape joy. All the way to heaven is heaven. Joy is a forgotten word in our vocabulary.

There is the joy of love, the love of one's neighbor.

There are ordinary joys and spiritual joys. The daily joys: going to bed, receiving a letter, a phone call, eating, experiencing another's joy, finding just the perfect gift for a friend, anticipating their joy; a visit from a friend, work well done, something accomplished, cold water when thirsty, sun after poor weather, the innocence of a child, gratitude; the joy of music, art, nature, the thrill of excitement, the joy of a

beautiful face, human presence, an old friend; feeling "life is good" (vita é buona), being known and loved; remembering and anticipating; the joy of traveling, coming home, being home; the joy of bread and wine, laughter and play.

There is the joy of faith, of presence, of forgiveness, of being born again. "Christ's joy is the sharing in the unfathomable joy, both divine and human, which is at the heart of Jesus Christ glorified." The deep quiet joy of the gift of goodness of life, of one's family; the joy of being loved, of being used, useful. The joyful mysteries of the rosary; the joy of the beatitudes; the joy of Easter and Pentecost, joy and glory. The Magnificat — hymn of joy. "Mater plena sanctae laetitia," cause of our joy. The joy of the martyrs, joy in the Holy Spirit. The radiant joy of holiness, the joy of Eucharist.

CANTICLE OF THE SUN

O most high, almighty, good Lord God, to You belong praise, glory, honor and all blessing!

Praised be my Lord God with all His creatures, and especially our brother the sun, who brings us the day and who brings us the light, fair is he and shines with a very great splendor: O Lord, he signifies to us You!

Praised be my Lord for our sister the moon, and for the stars, for which he has set clear and lovely in Heaven.

Praised be my Lord for our brother the wind, and for air and clouds, calms and all weather by which You uphold life in all creatures.

Praised be my Lord for our sister water, who is very serviceable unto us and humble and precious and clean.

Praised be my Lord for our brother fire, through whom You give us light in the darkness; and he is bright and pleasant and very mighty and strong.

Praised be my Lord for our mother the earth, which sustains us and keeps us, and brings forth divers fruits and flowers of many colors and grass.

Praise You and bless the Lord, and give thanks to Him and serve Him with great humility.

Praised be my Lord for all those who pardon one another for love's sake, and who endure weakness and tribulation.

Blessed are they who peaceably shall endure, for You, O most High, shall give them a crown.

Praised be my Lord for our sistèr, the death of the body, from which no man escapes. Woe to him who dies in mortal sin.

Blessed are they who are found walking by Your most holy will, for the second death shall have no power to do them harm.

Praise and bless my Lord, and thank him too, and serve him all, in great humility.

PRAY ALWAYS

"Pray continually and never lose heart" (Lk 18:1).

"Stay awake, praying at all times" (Lk 21:36).

"Pray constantly: and for all things give thanks to God" (1 Th 5:17).

"So that always and everywhere you are giving thanks to God" (Ep 5:20).

"Always be thankful (eucharistic)" (Col 3:15).

"Never say or do anything except in the name of the Lord Jesus, giving thanks to God the Father through him" (Col 3:17).

"Whatever you eat, whatever you drink, whatever you do at all, do it for the glory of God" (1 Co 10:31).

"In him, we live and move and have our being" (Ac 17:28).

"The mysteries of the kingdom of heaven are revealed to you . . . like a treasure hidden in a field . . . a net cast into the sea" (Mt 13).

"You must know, the kingdom of God is within you" (Lk 17:21).

"Unless you change and become like little children, you will never enter the kingdom of heaven" (Mt 18:3).

We rarely think of the ordinary actions of everyday — walking, sitting, traveling, sleeping, as prayer. Yet throughout the New Testament we are called to pray always, to enter into the presence of him who is with us in the dailyness of our every day. We are invited to be creative and receptive like little children, and by conscious experience to know, to rejoice in the kingdom of heaven existing within us, around us. "Well, I tell you: Look around you, look at the fields; already they are white, ready for harvest" (Jn 4:35). These are exercises in consciousness, preludes to prayer, practices of the presence of God, invitations to enter into the mind and heart, imagination and emotions of Jesus who shares, lives all our experiences with us. "I am with you always."

TRAVELING

"Now he is going before you to Galilee: it is there that you will see him." He goes before us; he goes with us in all of our journeyings. He has given us many parables of travelers: the Prodigal Son, the Jericho man, the narrow gate, the road which is wide and spacious. Take nothing for the journey other than a basket for bread, a cup for wine. "I am the Way" (Jn 6:1).

In traveling, new roads, new skies open to expand the mind and heart. One experiences a new freedom and freshness; something is reborn in one. We all delight in travel; few are immune to the wanderlust deep within. As Americans we are highly mobile and seem to be more comfortable in motion than at rest. We probably spend more time on wheels each day than we do at table. When there is nothing to do, many go out just for the drive, just to be in motion. Each year, with our new-found leisure, we do more and more traveling. Perhaps a spirituality of traveling will emerge or perhaps we will rediscover the ancient sense of pilgrimage which looks upon every road, every way as a holy one.

Traveling may not be recognized as a spiritual exercise, but it certainly can exercise, stretch the spirit! The world is a sacrament of God, the earth is the face of God. "All things are yours." Until recently, I had limited his country, the Holy Land, to Israel. But I have come more recently to recognize our country as his, all of it holy through his incarnation, redemption, all of it continued in holiness, through each one of us. The rivers, plains, the mountains, canyons, the desert, the ocean were made for me, create a new song, new prayer, new psalms in me in the awe, the wonder of gratitude and beauty. It is I who am traveled in and what I discover is what

is within me. "And God saw that it was good" —
the prayer of Genesis becomes mine in a new,
deeply rooted way. All of this was made for me,
all of it waiting to be seen, to be appreciated, to
be delighted in as only I could delight in it. All
of this sings its unique song in me. God speaks
to me on the way. He journeys in me; the inter-
state highways become a prayer. He stretches,
draws me to his dimensions, giving me new
eyes, new ears, a new tongue. "How infinitely
great is the power that he has exercised for us
believers." "The fullness of him who fills the
whole creation." Before the Grand Canyon, one
is awesomely conscious that "a thousand years
are as one day, and one day is as a thousand
years." "God! You are my Grand Canyon, my
Rocky Mountains. Your word is a Grand Canyon
which can be explored, wondered at endlessly,
infinitely. By becoming man, you have made all
of this yours; by your Ascension, you have lifted,
drawn all things with you, consecrating everything with your love, asking us to continue to
consecrate it in remembrance of you. God, you
are my ocean; there is so little of you that I can
see, so little that I can drink, that I can take into
myself."

SITTING

"He sat down (rested) on the seventh day after all the
work he had been doing. God blessed the seventh day
and made it holy, because on that day he had sat down
after all his work of creating" (Gn 2:2).

"When all is made new and the Son of Man sits on his
throne of glory, you will yourselves sit on twelve
thrones" (Mt 19:28).

> "He ascended into heaven and sits at the right hand of the Father" (Creed). "Living forever to intercede for all who come to God through him" (Heb 7:25).
>
> "Seeing the crowds, he went up the hill. There he sat down and was joined by his disciples" (Mt 5:1).
>
> "He then rolled up the scroll, gave it back to the assistant and sat down. And all eyes in the synagogue were fixed on him. Then he began to speak to them" (Lk 4:19).
>
> "Get them to sit down" (Lk 9:14). Miracle of the loaves.
>
> "So he sat down . . . He then took a little child, set him in front of them, put his arms 'round him, and said to them . . ." (Mk 9:35).
>
> "When evening came he was at table with the twelve disciples . . . Now as they were eating, Jesus took some bread . . ." (Mt 26:20).

Sitting is the posture of rest, of receptivity, of listening, of refreshment, of eating, of learning, of reading, of writing. Sitting is the posture of prayer, of Eucharist, of celebrating, feasting, of family and friendship.

How good it is to sit down when the work is done and time is not hanging over you.

How many the places, how many the ways in which we sit: sitting at work, at table, before the window, around the altar, alongside the hearth, at a bedside; to sit on a hill, upon the earth, under the shade of a tree. "I saw you under the fig tree" (Jn 2:48). Matthew was sitting by the customs house. The two blind men were sitting by the side of the road when Jesus passed by. Jesus was sitting at table when his feet were washed by Magdalene's tears and again when they were anointed for his burial. The apostles were sitting when Jesus washed their feet.

How renewing it is to sit in one's favorite chair, in the warmth of an old rocker, to sit and rock to the tune and rhythm of one's own heart, to rest, to think, to be, perhaps to dream, experiencing the quiet joy of being alive, healthy, graced, friended — the old Sunday afternoon feeling. It may be experiencing the transcendental quiet which comes in listening to music.

The Buddhists have a whole school of sitting meditation called "Zazen."

Much of our sitting is done in the car behind the driving wheel, in our mobile hermitage and cloister. This affords great privacy and seclusion for many people, alone on the crowded freeway. Once the mechanical concentration of driving is mastered, the inner spirit is free to reflect, to think, listen, pray. We seldom speak to our unknown companions on the road, our pilgrim fellow travelers, each on their own quest. We are each on our way into Jerusalem, sitting, not on a donkey, but on wheels. He sits up front with us. He is our constant companion, the one who breaks bread with us, the one who has promised, "I will never leave you alone" (Jn 14:18).

SLEEPING

"So Yahweh God made man fall into a deep sleep (Gn 3:21).

"He gives sleep to those he loves" (Ps 127:2).

"Now I can lie down and go to sleep and then awake, for Yahweh has hold of me" (Ps 3:5).

"In peace I lie down, and fall asleep at once, since you alone, Yahweh, make me rest secure" (Ps 4:8).

"The boat was almost swamped. But he was in the stern, his head on a cushion, asleep" (Mk 4:38).

"Peter and his companions were heavy with sleep, but they kept awake and saw his glory" (Lk 9:32).

"He came back a third time and said to them, 'You can sleep on now and take your rest. It is all over'" (Mk 14:41).

God does not like men who do not sleep at night. Sleep is one of God's most beautiful gifts to men. Sleep is the friend of man. Sleep is the friend of God. Peguy.

The joy of going to bed at night! The bed of conception, of birth, of suffering, of love, of death. The consolation of deep sleep. The sleep of ordinary tiredness, the sleep of exhaustion. The world of dream, and the unconscious. The great epic dreams I have had, the dreams of a child. The remembrance of things past, of roads traveled, people loved. The memory banks, treasuring the echoes of my entire life. Waking up at night and falling back to sleep. Awake in one's own dream.

The last moments of the day before falling asleep and the first moments of awakening from sleep are privileged times for prayer. The first, the last moments of sleep are sacramentals, holy moments, special times of consciousness. It is then that we are closest to the depths, the ground of our being.

Sleep is the time to rest with abundant peace and love in the heart of my God who watches and slumbers not. Blessed are you who sleep in the Lord. While I sleep he keeps the city. In the night of my sleep, he turns all of the earth upon her axis and fashions from darkness a new day of light. Sleep surrounds the heart of man with solitude. Sleep is the secret of being tireless.

In the night of sleep, man dreams and the Lord his God calls. Jacob dreamed the ladder.

Samuel heard the voice. A word was brought to Job. He caught a whisper of it during the vision of night when deep sleep fell upon him (Jb 4).

A messenger of God appeared to Joseph in sleep over and again. "Get up, take the child and his mother with you" (Mt 2:13).

"I sleep, yet my heart is awake" (Sg 5:2).

Then waking up to the joy, the excitement of a new day, a day which the Lord had made; in awe and wonder at a day yet to be breathed, filled with his Spirit.

> "I say this prayer to you, Yahweh,
> for at daybreak you listen for my voice;
> and at dawn I hold myself in readiness for you,
> I watch for you" (Ps 5:3).

WALKING

> "the sound of Yahweh God walking in the garden in the cool of the day" (Gn 3:8).
> "walk before me and be perfect" (Gn 17:1).
> "As he was walking by the sea . . . he said to them, follow me" (Mt 4:20).
> "he came toward them, walking on the lake."
> "follow in my footsteps" (Mt 10:39).
> "Walk while you have the light" (Jn 12:35).
> "'Walk in love as Christ loved us" (Ep 5:2).
> "Walk worthy of your vocation" (Ep 4:1).
> "Now as they talked this over, Jesus came up and walked by their side" (Lk 24:15).

God walked and talked with Adam and Eve in the cool of the evening. Jesus walked with his disciples the length and breadth of Galilee, Samaria, Judea. He walked the lake, the hills, the mountains and the plains, Mt. Hermon, Mt. Tabor, the Mount of Olives. He walked the streets of the towns and villages. Every walk of ours is an Emmaus Walk, he walks by our side, even though there is "something preventing us from recognizing him."

Walking is a kind of seeing, a kind of feeling, a kind of being present, rendering oneself present. There is a school of philosophy, the peripatetic followers of Aristotle, who developed their philosophy by walking up and down, back and forth, the body turning the mind over every facet of the subject. There is a school of meditation in Zen Buddhism which does its meditation through walking.

There is a way of knowing a place because you have put it under foot. You come on a place because you have footprinted it as carefully as if you had passed it through your hands. Grass and asphalt, wood and concrete, rock and sand give distinctive pressures to each footfall. Walking brings with it a gentleness, a calmness, an openness, a freedom. Weather brings a newness to each walk — rain walks, sun walks, wind walks, snow walks. And the sounds and echoes of walking! It is in walking that one discovers the moods and music, the voices and silences of the city and woods, the river and lake.

The most natural form of movement is the human step, man's pace — three miles an hour, thirty a day! How long it took to learn the rhythm of lifting our legs, swinging our arms! Each person has his own unique stride, her own personal rhythm. The whole body responds. The arms dance to the feet, the breath fills the chest, becomes deeper and fuller. Each person treads the earth distinctively, on heel or ball, or both together.

We walk for the sheer joy of walking, to stretch ourselves to our fullest dimensions. We walk on top of the earth or on the bottom like a fly on the ceiling held by gravity alone. The earth holds us to herself with the gravity of love.

I wonder how mother earth responds to the the touch of all of our feet: barefoot and sandals, boots and slippers, work shoes and play shoes, the heaviness and gentleness of feet! The first step of the child and the last step of the dying man; the Springtime of walking and the Autumn of walking; the Calvary walk, the Ascension walk. All walking is a blessing, a prayer. Walk in the newness of life. Walk in faith and in the spirit. Watch and listen for his footsteps.

DARKNESS ... IN DARKNESS
Faith, Prayer, Communion of Saints

Many of God's gifts to us remain hidden and unseen simply because they are so near to us. He tells us again and again, "Unless you become like little children . . ."

Darkness
  Fire
    Food
      even Feet

are invitations to pause and be drawn inward, to be caught and enchanted by the real beyond words and symbols, to experience the preludes to prayer and adoration.

Find yourself a room where there is total darkness, no cracks of light — a windowless room or auditorium, stage, storage room.

Seat yourself as comfortably as possible. Put out all the lights. Block out any cracks of light. Close your eyes, tune into your breathing, check your tension points, go into your deep center and be as totally quiet as possible.

Now open your eyes and experience the total darkness.

Be aware of your first feelings of the darkness. It is strange to open your eyes and to see nothing before you. In our contemporary culture filled with artificial light, total darkness is almost never experienced. We are deprived of the rich human experience of night. Most have lost the knowledge of stars, the mystery of twilight, of dawn . . . Light creates distance; darkness creates nearness and intimacy. Darkness removes space and time. All darkness is the same. This is the darkness that "covered the deep" in creation. This is the darkness that covered us in the womb, the darkness we knew as a child, the darkness which lies ahead of us in death and the tomb . . . When our eyes cannot function, the sense of touch intensifies. Be aware of the total alertness of your whole body. Be conscious of your body space, a delicate radar which extends beyond your body sensing what is close to you.

Now raise your hand and hold it in front of your face with your eyes wide open . . . You know it is there but you see nothing!

Darkness overcomes our self-consciousness; we may feel more free to speak.

Now feel free to express any feeling you are experiencing about the darkness . . . What must be the anguish of the person born blind . . .

Now as quietly as possible turn to the person on either side and look into their face . . . You know they are there but you look into nothing! or they may be looking the other way!

(If there is adequate space and no obstacles to run into or trip over) —

As quietly as possible stand up and begin very slowly and gently to move around the room. If you feel nervous and want to laugh, let yourself breathe deeply and return to your peace center. You will feel others brush by you as you move by them. This is what we do all the time, especially with those we know . . . Now sit down again wherever you are, and reflect upon this experience of walking in the darkness, not knowing who walks with you.

We think of God as Light, but God is also Darkness. Often in darkness we can sense him more near than in the light. Light creates distance; darkness, closeness and intimacy. As darkness encompasses me completely, so does God. "No one has ever seen God, it is only the Son, who is nearest to the Father's heart, who has made him known." Only faith can overcome the darkness which envelops our mind and reason. In the darkness we cannot see our hand an inch before our eyes nor the face which is next to our own. Wonderful are our eyes, but how little they "see." They catch only the light reflected from another surface. In darkness we "see" so much more deeply. In daylight we hardly recognize a face at fifty feet; at night we can see the distant galaxy!

Who was that who passed you in the dark, the one you brushed against with your left shoulder? It could have been anyone. It could have been him! It was! It is!

Your eyes tell you that there is no one in the room. Yet you know it is filled with people. You cannot see prayer but whenever you pray you know that you are connected with everyone who prays. Whenever one prays he is in Christ and Christ is in him and with him is the communion and community of saints — "That they may be one as we are one. With me in them and you in me" (Jn 17:22).

Now close your eyes as the lights are turned on. Begin to share your experience with the person you find next to you.

MEDITATION ON FOOD
Exercise on Eucharist and Community

Eating in all world religions is a holy and sacred action. One of the oldest, longest retained of religious customs is the one of praying before and after meals. Food Prayers are our most consistent act of thanksgiving (or complaint! — Lament Psalms are not uncommon in the prayer of the Hebrew Scriptures). Until the mid-fifties, in most religious communities and seminaries, meals were eaten in silence accompanied by spiritual reading. This remains the practice in some monastic communities.

It is not surprising that this tradition of so many centuries became extinct almost over night. People forget. The language of a tradition is no longer understood. The practice is discarded. But deep human values and truths do not remain buried for long. One discovers the "new" only to realize later that it is as old, as young as humanity itself.

In Japan and India, I rediscovered the ancient value of the silent meal and the meditation of food. The tea ceremony of the Japanese is a contemplative action which comes close to the reverence, depth, simplicity of a Trappist Liturgy. The prayers before meals in a Buddhist monastery are twice as long as the time for consuming one's food in silence. Before a Hindu eats his food he first places it before the altar and in prayer offers it to the deity. Viewing this immediately recalled to my memory the Old Testament "peace offerings," the sacrifice of communion, a meal of joy in which the best portion was offered, burnt for the Lord, the rest eaten by the offerers. Thus the idea of food prolonging the ritual sacrifice and communion with God.

All food is "manna" from God. All eating can be a communion with him, the Giver, the Lover of all. Our food is not blessed in the quick sign of the cross or the too-hurried words of "grace." The sign, the words do not make the meal holy. They are but a recognition of the truth that the action one is about to perform *is* already holy. Grace is an act of reverence before that which is holy, a gift from him who is All Holy. Prayer is a recognition that he who eats is holy, a son of God, son of his Father, anticipating the heavenly banquet.

Let us begin.

Everyone is seated at the dinner table. This meditation will be appreciated best if the meal is a Sunday or festive one; and if everyone as well as the table is "dressed" for the occasion. We do too much "eating," too little "dining." No prayer is "recited." The act of our eating will be our prayer.

Close your eyes, tune into your breathing, check your tension points, go into your peace center and begin to relish what you are about to eat. Begin to welcome your "manna" with a joyful, thankful smile.

Open your eyes and let your eyes "feast" on what you are about to eat. Use your silverware or be free to use your fingers. Little children know how to enjoy their food; they usually play with it for a while.

Savour whatever you eat as long as you can. Let it liquify before you swallow it. Be aware that this is a holy act, so holy that Jesus uses it as the occasion for performing his miracle, giving us his deepest words, leaving forever his Body and Blood as our food and drink.

Listen to your food, let it speak its word, its secret, its history to you. Enjoy the color, the texture, the size, shape, the sound. All the world is present upon your table. How many unseen hands have labored to fill your plate!

What you are eating is letting go of its life in order to enter into your life. Now the food becomes you. Family table . . . Father's house. Mother's flour, Father's grapes . . bread — creation of woman's hand . . . wine — work of man's hands. "Give us this day our daily bread." God so loved the world that he became food, our bread and wine. He changes bread and wine into himself . . . So are we to become what he is. We change bread and wine into our body and blood. When we eat his Body and drink his Blood, he changes us into himself. "I live, no longer I, but Christ lives in me."

Sharing the same table is the sign of friendship, of love, of sharing the same life. To eat together is to receive one another . . .

When the Body and Blood of Christ is rendered present, we who are the whole Christ are rendered present. When we receive him, we receive all who are one in him.

"If you love me, *feed* my sheep."

When you have finished eating, close your eyes and remain in your center; be aware that when your eating is finished, the processing of your body is but begun. Be aware of the mystery of your new life unfolding.

Now open your eyes and share your thanksgiving with one another.

WASHING OF FEET

Exercise of the 'Sign of Discipleship'

This is a meditation exercise taught by Christ himself. The whole Christian Community is invited to experience and celebrate this "sign" in the solemn Liturgy of Holy Thursday. It is a sign that some of the early Fathers of the Church looked upon as a Sacrament. Many have watched this ceremony from the edge of the crowd; few have participated in this liturgical experience directly, even though we are each under his command, "If I, then, your Lord and Master,

have washed your feet, you should wash each other's feet!" This is a very awkward and embarrassing command. We can readily identify with Peter and cry out, "Never! You shall never wash my feet." But in the next breath we are confronted with the awesome response of Jesus to Peter: "If I do not wash you, you can have nothing in common with me!"

This exercise is best celebrated with a family-size group in the setting of the Eucharistic Liturgy, as Christ himself celebrated it.

Everyone comes with bare feet.

Let the group be seated in a circle or circles, with a basin, pitcher and towels in the center. The Liturgy of the Word is that of Holy Thursday. Each one prays silently for a deep spirit of prayer and humility to overcome the natural nervousness and reluctance before such an experience.

The priest reads the Gospel of John, Chapter 13:1-11: "It was before the festival of the Passover . . . (Jerusalem translation) . . . though not all of you are." Here the priest pauses, takes off his chasuble and stole, and takes the basin, pitcher and towel to the person on his right.

Let everyone close his eyes, tune into his breathing, go into his deep center to experience fully the mystery and symbolism of this action of Christ which he is about to have done to him and which he will do to another.

The priest with prayer and reverence washes both feet of the person before whom he kneels. As he dries each foot, he kisses it in an act of humility. Then the priest gives the towel and water to the person whose feet he has just washed and that person in turn washes the feet of the next person in the same manner. This continues around, with the last person in the circle washing the feet of the priest.

No music or singing is necessary. Let each person be in prayer, listen to the sounds of the washing and remember that Last Supper. Before he took bread into his hands, he took the feet of his disciples!

When the priest's feet have been washed, he puts on his vestments and continues the Gospel of John 13:

12-18: "When he had washed their feet and put on his clothes again he went back to the table. Do you understand . . . Now that you know this, happiness will be yours if you behave accordingly."
Let us meditate . . .

"Do *you* understand what *I* have done to you?" Who washed your feet? It could have been anyone's hands . . . It could have been his! . . . It was! He has no other hands! Whose feet did you wash? It could have been anyone's feet. It could have been his feet! . . . It was! He has no other feet! He has no other hands, no other feet, except yours and mine!

Before he took bread into his hands to change it into his body, he first took the feet of his disciples! What an "anointing" that must have been! And how necessary, if these feet were ever to follow in his footsteps. "How beautiful are the feet of those who carry the glad tidings of the Good News" (Isaiah). Could they ever forget the way in which he held, washed and kissed their feet! What strength they must have drawn from the remembrance of that moment, when at other moments their feet were weary and bleeding from the hard roads of their missionary journeys.

One wonders about his hands and feet. What were they like, those hands and feet which were to be nailed to the cross before the sun set the next day!

How blessed are the feet of those who follow him! Now it is the touch of our feet which makes the ground holy. Take off your shoes and the earth becomes holy! Follow me, follow my footprints, the path which my feet have created, and for which your feet have now been anointed.

Now share your response with your community.

The community then "footprints" its way to the Eucharistic Table to continue the Liturgy.

MEDITATION ON FIRE

Meditation on fire is the first of the meditations which the Church teaches us in the Liturgy of the Easter Vigil. But this is too rich a meditation to be limited to one night. Every sanctuary lamp, every candle enkindled on the altar is an invitation to remember, to re-celebrate the mystery, the sacrament, the prayer of fire.

Gather the group around the fireplace or the bonfire in the open air.

Declare the silence and invite each one to watch for the spark or flame which ignites the fire. The wonder of a spark struck from flint, fire leaping from a stone!

No directed relaxation is necessary. Fire itself quiets and moves one into the deeper silences within.

The taming of fire was man's first conquest, the Prometheus stealing fire from the gods. Fire is man's oldest ally, never irreversibly a friend, too easily an enemy. Fire is never totally domesticated; it owns itself, retaining its unpredictable wildness and destructiveness. It can be controlled but not changed. Whatever it touches, it turns into itself. Yet it cannot exist by itself; it must adhere, inhere in something. Fire is transformative; it creates something new, shapes old things into ever new possibilities. Fire is man's great servant, his most powerful and creative tool. Man cannot touch fire, yet learning to harness it has given him his civilization. The story of civilization and culture is the story of fire from hearth to outer space, from flint spark to atomic bomb.

Now let each one speak aloud his stream of consciousness which the fire draws out of him: poetry, song, prayer, Scripture.

"I have come to cast fire on the earth and I would that it be enkindled." .. ..

"And something appeared to them that seemed like tongues of fire; these separated and came to rest on the head of each of them."

". . . to Jesus' heart all burning with fervent love for men."

Pillar of fire by night.

"With a live coal he touched my mouth" (Is 6:6).

God as consuming fire!

"Enkindle in us the fire of your divine love."

"The flash of it is a flash of fire,
a flame of Yahweh himself.
Love no flood can quench,
no torrents drown" (Canticle of Canticles).

102

Three young men in fiery furnace.

Fire of temptation. Fire of purification.

"Be worthy of the flame consuming you" (Claudel).

Paschal Candle, Sanctuary Lamp, Altar Candles, Prayer Candle, Baptismal Candle, Marriage Candle, Vow Candle, Ordination Candle.

Quality of fire is conditioned by the quality of its material.

Sacred fire — the fire of sacrifice, fire of incense — spiritualizing of the offering.

"For Yahweh your God is a consuming fire, a jealous God" (Dt 4:24).

"Everyone will be salted by fire" (Mk 9:50).

"He will baptize you with the Holy Spirit and fire" (Mt 3:11).

Fire of the Sun, the stars, the candle, the match, the human heart.

OBJECT MEDITATION
Exercise in Sacramentality

"Unless you become like little children . . ."

What is so lovely about little children is their sense of wonder and joyful imagination. They animate, personalize, companion everything in their lives. Too soon we grow old and "have eyes that do not see, ears that do not hear, and hands that cannot touch." To let our sense of wonder die is to close ourselves to the sacred and sacramental.

Let us begin:

Go outside and let some natural object choose you; a stone, a flower, blade of grass, weed, feather, grains of sand, pine cone, seashell, leaf — anything which you can hold in your hand that exists in its natural state and is not processed or manufactured.

Take the same posture as in the exercise in adoration. Eyes closed, tune into your breathing, relax tension points, go into your deep center. Become aware of the air at your fingertips and now of the object resting in your hand. Without touching it with your fingers, become aware of how it makes itself felt in your hand: the surface it covers; its weight; its warmth or coolness; its texture. Now reverently begin to explore your object with your fingers. How differently you come to know through touch. Realize how your eyes cannot see its firmness or softness; its flexibility or resistance: its roughness or smoothness. Be aware of how it changes through your touch, takes on your warmth, contracts or expands.

Now raise your object to your cheek, notice how different the touch of your cheek is from that of your hand.

Pass your object across your ear and listen to its sound. Now draw it close to your nose and detect its scent. Touch it to your lips and, if you wish, taste it with the tip of your tongue. Now lower your object gently and reverently to your lap.

Everything that is has a language, has something to say. Everything that is has value and meaning. Everything that is has a secret and is a mystery. Everything that is has a history, has come a long way. Everything that is is on a journey, has a destiny. Everything that is has something to share, something to give, something to say, something to receive. Everything that is has something to speak to you about yourself, to teach you something that nothing else could teach you.

Unless you become like a little child you will not understand, you will not receive the gift and wisdom that is waiting for you. So in your imagination become the size of your object, go into its center, learn its history, experience something of its destiny. Or let your object become your size and take it into your center. Give yourself to your object, be with it, go with it for a little while on its journey, listen to it, learn from it, discover its name . . . (15 minutes).

Now it is time to say goodbye to your friend. What makes it so important is the time you have wasted with it. Express your gratitude to it in some tangible way.

Now lift your object closer to your face so that as you open your eyes all that you will see is your new friend. . . . When you wish, begin to write from your stream of consciousness.

This is the kind of prayer that fills the psalms. From the experiences of everyday things the mind and heart is lifted to him from whom all things flow. Everything is a gift of God's love, goodness, wonder and beauty. Everything can be a sacrament of God, an epiphany, a transparency of his presence. There is nothing in creation or man's experience that has not been an occasion of man's recognizing the power and presence of God. Our Lord took bread and wine, water and oil, human word and gesture and made of them encounters with himself.

The sacraments and psalms can teach us how to pray and how to discern his presence and love in all the things of our day. If we do not recognize him, "the very stones will cry out."

If we do not let our hearts grow hard as our arteries can, we will be prayed in constantly and like him we will each day eternalize the lilies of the field and the birds of the air. What have you gathered into your heart? What are you bringing to his kingdom? So much waits for you; so much waits to be returned to him in you.

HAND MEDITATION
Exercise in Community

Same posture as in other meditations — eyes closed, hands resting in lap, palms up, tune into your breathing, relax tension points and go into your center.

Become aware of the air at your fingertips, between your fingers, on the palm of your hand. Experience the fullness, strength and maturity of your hands. Think of your hands, think of the most unforgettable hands you have known—the hands of your father, your mother, your grandparents. Remember the oldest hands that have rested in your hands. Think of the hands of a new-born child, your nephew or niece — of the incredible beauty, perfection, delicacy in the hands of a child. Once upon a time your hands were the same size.

Think of all that your hands have done since then. Almost all that you have learned has been through your hands — turning yourself over, crawling and creeping, walking and balancing yourself; learning to hold something for the first time; feeding yourself, washing and bathing, dressing yourself. At one time your greatest accomplishment was tying your own shoes.

Think of all the learning your hands have done and how many activities they have mastered, the things they have made. Remember the day you could write your own name.

Our hands were not just for ourselves but for others. How often they were given to help another. Remember all the kinds of work they have done, the tiredness and aching they have known, the cold and the heat, the soreness and the bruises. Remember the tears they have wiped away, our own or another's, the blood they have bled, the healing they have experienced. How much hurt, anger and even violence they have expressed, and how much gentleness, tenderness and love they have given.

How often they have been folded in prayer; a sign both of their powerlessness and of their power. Our father and mother guided these hands in the great symbolic language of our hands — the sign of the cross, the striking of our breast, the handshake, the wave of the hand in "hello" or "goodbye."

There is a mystery which we discover in the hand of a woman or the hand of a man that we love. There are the hands of a doctor, a nurse, an artist, a conductor, a priest, hands which you can never forget.

Now raise your right hand slowly and gently place it over your heart. Press more firmly until your hand picks up the beat of your heart, that most mysterious of all human sounds, one's own heartbeat, a rhythm learned in the womb from the heartbeat of one's mother. Press more firmly for a moment and then release your hand and hold it just a fraction from your clothing. Experience the warmth between your hand and your heart. Now lower your hand to your lap very carefully as if it were carrying your heart. For it does. When you extend your hand to another, it is not just bone and skin, it is your heart. A handshake is the real heart transplant.

Think of all the hands that have left their imprint on you. Fingerprints and handprints are heartprints that can never be erased. The hand has its own memory. Think of all the places that people carry your handprints and all the people who bear your heartprint. They are indelible and will last forever.

Now without opening your eyes extend your hands on either side and find another hand. Do not simply hold it but explore it and sense the history and mystery of this hand. Let your hand speak to it and let it listen to the other. Try to express your gratitude for this hand stretched out to you in the dark and then bring your hand back again to your lap. Experience the presence of that hand lingering upon your hand. The afterglow will fade but the print is there forever.

Whose hand was that? It could have been any hand; it could have been his hand. It was. He has no other hands than ours.

Now begin to write out of your stream of consciousness.

ADORATION
"I am with you."

Prayer essentially is to become present to oneself, to God, to all of reality. It is not easy to become present to oneself, to be fully con-

scious, to be totally awake. Practice, training, exercise are necessary to discover oneself, to receive the gift of oneself. We are so caught up in events and with the people in our lives that we rarely take time to consider our own selves to be worth any time at all. To take time for ourselves also triggers some guilt in us. Yet only if we are free to "waste" time on ourselves are we truly free. The closest reality to God that one will ever experience is oneself. Each of us is an existence of God, a presence of Christ, a sacrament of the church, a gift to the world. Bonhoeffer expresses it: "if you refuse to be with yourself alone you are rejecting Christ's call to you."

Each of us needs a "peace center," a place where we can be most ourselves, a home that welcomes us no matter how we are or what we have done. It can be a cottage, a park, a mountain, woods, a chapel. As life goes on we find different peace centers. When we most need our geographical peace center, however, time and the situation sometimes render it impossible. We are compelled to create our peace center within ourselves. Jesus had to leave Nazareth, yet he always carried it within himself. Each of us has to create our hermitage and oasis within, our Nazareth, our Bethany.

Let us begin!

Close your eyes and sit as erect as possible, your feet flat on the ground and your hands on your lap, palms up, without touching each other. A straight-backed chair is best, lounge chairs actually make the body restless.

Begin to be aware of your breathing. Tune into the sensation of your whole body breathing. Let your breathing relax all of you.

Check the tension points. Press your eyes tightly for a few seconds, and release immediately and this will free your forehead of its intensity. Let your head tip forward in slow motion and the tension muscles of your neck will relax. Let your jaw loose and let it take a gentle yawn.

Begin to experience your whole body smiling. Feel how good it is to be here, now, and have nothing to do but *be*. Be aware of the mystery of your own breath. The Hebrews thought of their breath as the breath of God; it did not belong to them, it was his. His presence in them made them alive. When God took back his breath, death returned their body to earth. Be conscious that you breathe in the Spirit so that you can send forth the Word.

Now without moving your hands begin to become aware of the air at your fingertips, between your fingers, on the palms of your hands. It is always there, the delicate touch of the atmosphere and the gentle pressure of gravity. But we are not aware of this because all day our senses are drawing us out of ourselves and we rarely are this present to ourselves.

Become aware of the openness of your hands. This is the oldest gesture of prayer known to man, to man deeply conscious of the mystery of his own existence, his hands extended in offering and in reception, to give and to accept. When man is quiet and alone he is always close to wonder. He knows that he is in the Presence of Someone beyond himself, the world, and all others. The man of faith calls this Presence God, God who speaks to man and reveals himself. God spoke to Moses and gave him his name — "I am who am and as who I am I will be with you." This promise became flesh in Christ who speaks his "I am" in us and calls us to echo his words in return, "I am with you," "We are with You."

"Unless you become like little children, you cannot enter the kingdom." "The Kingdom of heaven is within you." Now go into your center where you are most yourself; to the room where you can pray to your Father in secret, "to the light which is at the still-point of the turning world," the inmost self of the psalms, the holy of holies where we meet Christ in Eucharist. Experience how good it is to be you and to hear yourself able to say "I am," "I am me," and, "It is good to be the me that I am."

Let the Word of God echo itself in you:

"In him we live and move and have our being."

"Do you not know that you are the temple of God and that his spirit lives in you?"

"If you but knew the gift of God and who it is that speaks to you."

"I will come to you and my Father will come to you and we will make our home in you."

"All things are yours, and you are Christ's and Christ is God."

"You are dead and your life is hidden with Christ in God."

"I live now, not I, but Christ lives in me."

Be at peace in the depths of your heart which he has created in his own image. There is a holy well within each of us. Let this well of peace and of love sink deeper. Remember the cumulative deposit of his presence in you through his Word, Sacrament and the people sent into your life.

Wait, be patient with God. Be like a faithful hound at the foot of his master, a beggar at the door of a cathedral, a fisherman before the ocean. The Spirit can touch in many ways, through our mind, imagination, memory, affectivity. He can influence the way we remember the past or anticipate the future. He can influence our desires, our convictions, our moving in one way or another.

Listen to him call you by name, asking you the old, ever new question he asks of all his disciples:

"Whom do you say I am?"
"Do you love me?"
"What do you want, for what are you searching?"
"What do you want me to do for you?"
"Do you believe me?"

He may come to us in an event of the Gospel, a mystery of the rosary, a station of the cross. To each of us Jesus gives a unique fragment of his Gospel which becomes a seed and core for our way of discipleship. There are certain words of power that call us as do no other words. It is the Holy Spirit who gives us the Christian "mantra." It is he who enables us to pray and to take the Word from the level of thought down into the heart where it lives itself with every heart beat. A man can be transformed by one Word filled by the Spirit. "Father;" Lord;" "Jesus;" Mercy; Peace; Light; Life; Truth; Glory; Holy; Come; Go.

When the time available is finished let us express our inner prayer of thanksgiving for what he has done in us. Let us become aware of our presence extending beyond our bodies, rippling out and interpenetrating the presence of the others with us in his presence. Let our presence and consciousness expand beyond the walls of the room into and across our city, state, nation, world, and know that in him we are stretched to the fullness of his dimensions, of his consciousness and heart.

Then in slow motion open your eyes and continuing in silence, write out of your stream of consciousness.

ABANDONMENT
Exercise in Listening to One's Own Prayer.

The prayers we say most frequently are the most difficult prayers to pray. There is no area of life where illusion is more dangerous and easy than in prayer. We can be *saying* prayers long after we have ceased praying. The psalms are not prayers in themselves; scripture is not prayer; reading is not prayer. The response in faith, hope and love is prayer, not the reading or saying.

Let us begin:

PRAYER OF ABANDONMENT
Father,
I abandon myself into your hands;
do with me what you will.
Whatever you may do, I thank you:
I am ready for all, I accept all.
Let only your will be done in me,
and in all your creatures —
I wish no more than this, O Lord.

Into your hands I commend my soul;
I offer it to you with all the love of my heart,
for I love you, Lord,
and so need to give myself,
to surrender myself into your hands,
without reserve,
and with boundless confidence,
For you are my Father.

Read this *Prayer Of Abandonment*. It is Charles de Foucauld's personalized translation of the "Our Father." We do not pray until the words of a prayer become our own thought, feeling and action. What part of this prayer do you find most easy to pray? What is most difficult? I find it easiest to say, "I most need to give myself." I am finding it most difficult to say, "I love you, Lord." I can almost hear him exclaim, "You what!?"

I remember being on a panel with a Rabbi and hearing him say with sadness, "We have had two thousand years of Christian 'love.' Let's have no more of it." I have so carelessly betrayed the word "love" that I am afraid to say it.

The other expression I find difficult to pray is "Father." I begin to realize how little I let him be Father to me. In my arrogant and blind independence I know that my life is far from being centered in him.

The greatest danger in each of us is the distance between our eyes and our feet, our vision and our behavior, our thoughts and our activity. We can see the distant mountain in a fraction of a moment but it may take our whole life to climb it. We may know the answer to our problem but we can postpone acknowledging it for years. Even Foucauld could say, "My words are stronger than my heart."

Meditation on each of these thoughts and discernment of the reality, or lack thereof, supporting my words is the first stage in praying this prayer.

Second Stage:

Read and contemplate this prayer again but instead of addressing it to the Father, put in the names of the people with whom you live and work each day — John, Mary, Tom, Jane, etc. "I abandon myself into your hands . . ." How does this affect your prayer? Is it possible to give yourself to another in this way? What do you find most possible to say? What do you find most difficult?

What I find most difficult is, "Do with me what *you will*. Whatever you may do, *I thank you*. What is easiest is the last line, "For you are mine."

The terrifying test of our prayer is expressed in the Last Judgment, Matthew 25, "As long as you have not done this to the least of these my brothers, you have not done it to me." Jesus has identified himself with every man and, as with Paul, at any moment a light may come and we hear his voice, "I am Jesus and you are persecuting me."

How could we dare trust ourselves to another person so totally? How could we trust ourselves? Would it be good for them; would it be good for us? What would happen if we did? Would it be human, let alone Christian to do so? What would happen if someone entrusted himself totally to me? It is not altogether rare. Every friendship, every love moves in that direction.

117

We forget the awesome creative power we have in each other's lives. When someone trusts us totally and completely, they compel us to grow, to measure up to their love, to become what they believe us to be. Each of us has incredible power to enable each other to grow and to become a new person in the measure we believe in them, hope in them and love them into a new fullness which they never recognized in themselves. We discover a new self-concept through the love and trust another has in us; we are born again. We are humbled, frightened by such love, such trust. We are more comfortable with our enemies and strangers who cannot ask from us. The more honest we are with ourselves, the more we realize that we do *not* pray like this; we *cannot* pray like this.

Third Stage:

Only Jesus can pray like this, only Jesus can say "Father" with the fullest depth of his being. We cannot pray the *Prayer Of Abandonment*. This is Jesus' prayer alone. But if we desire, Jesus will teach us and enable us to pray his prayer.

Now listen to Jesus pray this prayer to you. In place of the word "Father" and "Lord," put your own name and take time to try to listen to the way Jesus says your name, the way he calls you. He says your name as no one has ever said or will ever say your name. He calls you as only he who made you can call you, and he compels you to experience something of the fullness he has implanted in you because you are his image and likeness.

Listen to the depths of his word to you.

118

This is the prayer of your creation, of your being called into existence. This is the prayer of his baptism of you. This is the prayer of Eucharist which he prays and does each day in you. This is the prayer of Ordination, of Profession, of Marriage, of Discipleship. This is the prayer of the saints that renders Christ present in every generation in every situation of life.